INTEGRATIVE GESTALT
PRACTICE

INTEGRATIVE GESTALT PRACTICE

PRACTICE

Transforming Our Ways of Working with People

Mikael Sonne and
Jan Tønnesvang

KARNAC

Originally published in Danish as *Integrativ Gestalt Praksis: kompleksitet og helhed i arbejdet med mennesker* by Hans Reitzels Forlag, 2013.

This revised and elaborated edition first published in English in 2015 by Karnac Books Ltd
118 Finchley Road, London NW3 5HT

British Library Cataloguing in Publication Data

A C.I.P. for this book is available from the British Library

ISBN 978 1 78220 251 6

Edited, designed and produced by The Studio Publishing Services Ltd
www.publishingservicesuk.co.uk
e-mail: studio@publishingservicesuk.co.uk

Printed in Great Britain

www.karnacbooks.com

CONTENTS

ACKNOWLEDGEMENTS

Special thanks go to psychologist James Hammink, with whom we have founded and developed integrative gestalt practice (IGP), and to our students and course participants who, by taking part in our experiments, contributed to the theoretical and practical development of IGP.

*With memories of inspiring and vitalising companionship
with our dear friend and colleague, Todd Burley (1945–2014)*

ABOUT THE AUTHORS

Mikael Sonne (b. 1951) is a psychologist specialising in psychotherapy and a supervisor at postgraduate level. He is the founder and director of Aarhus Gestalt Institute and a co-founder of the Centre for Integrative Gestalt Practice (IGP). Mikael is head of a postgraduate gestalt training programme for psychologists and head of an educational programme in personal leadership development for executives. In his practice as a psychologist, Mikael works with coaching, supervision, organisational development, and therapy. He is a guest lecturer on IGP in the Department of Psychology and Behavioural Sciences at Aarhus University. He is a leading member of the Danish gestalt therapy forum. Mikael Sonne has a background as a psychologist in psychiatric settings, received gestalt training from Erving and Miriam Polster at the Gestalt Training Center in San Diego, from Natasha Mann, Barrie Simmons, Todd Burley, Gary Yontef and others, and from Bob Moore on meditation and energy work.

Jan Tønnesvang, PhD (b. 1963) is a psychologist and professor of psychology at the Department of Psychology and Behavioural Sciences at Aarhus University. He is head of the research unit for Integrative Psychology and the Network for Integrative Vitalising

Psychology, Intervention and Bildung. He is a co-founder of the Centre for Integrative Gestalt Practice (IGP), and a cofounder of the Integral Network, Integraldenmark.org. Jan is a trained gestalt therapist and combines his academic and practical interests in efforts to develop IGP and integral vitalising psychology (IVP) as a combined holistic approach to understand and work with human Bildung processes. He has developed a strategy called theoretically based practice development aimed at developing vitalising environments in educational, psychological, and organisational settings. He has authored and co-authored a large number of scientific articles and books.

*   *   *

The Centre for Integrative Gestalt Practice (www.gestalt.dk) was founded and developed in a collaboration involving the two authors of this book and psychologist James Hammink, who is a gestalt-trained practising psychologist and associated with the growth centre in Nr. Snede, Denmark. Together, the three founders have worked with and developed IGP. In recent years, these development efforts have also involved international collaboration in The Aarhus Research Group in Gestalt with the late Professor Todd Burley from Loma Linda University in Los Angeles and Alexandr Eremeev, MD, who is director of The Gestalt Therapy Development Society in Kyrgyzstan.

Introduction

The background for the book

In their book, *Gestalt Therapy Integrated*, Erving and Miriam Polster (1973) write that psychotherapy is too good to be limited to the sick. Their statement is especially true for psychotherapies that address fundamental existential issues and life challenges without reducing people to a set of symptoms and psychotherapy to manualised methods. There are still a handful of these psychotherapies around, and they are all faced with the challenge of today's demand for quick-fix solutions and tendency towards evidence mixing. Psychotherapies that are concerned with complexities and wholeness in people's lives are uncomfortable with having to work within narrow, bureaucratically defined criteria for what constitutes the good life, what is worth pursuing, and what the marketplace considers the right methods. They want to fix, and they like to mix, but they prefer treating the focus of their work—the individual(s) in question—as the point of departure and ethical point of reference for what needs to be done, and how. They do not define themselves in accordance with a specific method, but, rather, with a set of fundamental psychological and anthropological principles that enable them to understand and work with personal life challenges, sufferings, development, and growth in a more general sense, in a variety of contexts and with a variety of methodological strategies, depending on what the case calls for.

Gestalt therapy is one such approach. It is characterised by the general psychological and anthropological principles that it applies in its efforts to gain a holistic understanding of human life processes and their unfolding in social, cultural, and societal contexts. It rests on an underlying field theory that considers both the human organism as a whole and all the aspects of the social, cultural, and societal environment of which that organism is a part. In addition, it rests on a view of development which acknowledges that, throughout life, the individual is brought into situations that contain, on the one hand, the potential for growth and development and, on the other hand, the potential for stagnation, psychological imbalance, and disorder. What is of particular interest to the gestalt practitioner is how the individual as a human organism in its life expressions is enmeshed (for better and worse) in its environment and how it creates meaning, coherence, and a sense of direction in this environment by means of gestalt formation. In this sense, the gestalt approach may be said to rest on an organismic–dialectic understanding, which renders it compatible, for example, with current neurophysiological (Damasio, 1999) research approaches and theories of self-determination (Deci & Ryan, 2000).

With this book, we aim to demonstrate how the field theory and the concepts of the human organism and gestalt formation that characterise the gestalt approach can form the basis for the generation of psychological knowledge, understanding, and interventions on several levels and in a variety of contexts. As is evident from the title of the book, we have labelled our approach integrative gestalt practice (IGP).

IGP is about applying and developing the theoretical principles of the gestalt approach (concerning the field, the organism, and the dynamics of gestalt formation) in an effort to work in a non-reductionist manner with the wholes (individuals, groups, organisations etc.) that we address. This may take a practical as well as a theoretical form. In *practical* IGP work, it means taking in a broad-spectrum, yet systematic, view of the larger whole that surrounds the gestalt formation process in a practical context—for example, in therapy, supervision, and organisational development. In *theoretical* IGP work, it means seeking to incorporate and integrate knowledge from other practical, theoretical, and empirical approaches within the framework of IGP. The book will address both the practical and the theoretical side of IGP.

For some years, we have investigated and discussed which elements of the gestalt theory and method need to be rephrased or revised to enable the approach to manifest itself in the future market of psychological approaches with the success that it deserves. On the one hand, it is interesting to note how certain new concepts, for example ACT (acceptance and commitment therapy), coherence therapy, and mindfulness approaches, very successfully apply conceptual principles and elements that already exist in the gestalt approach. At the same time, it is thought stimulating to see how the gestalt approach itself is virtually absent from the treatment-orientated and academic psychological environments. There are probably several reasons for this. One reason might be Perls' rebellious style as reflected in his statements and his gestalt therapy practice; this style was probably appropriate for his time, characterised as it was by youth rebellion and other emancipation movements, whereas later times have rejected it as being too unambiguously anti-systems, anti-intellectual, and anti-conformist. Another reason could be that the classic gestalt book, *Gestalt Therapy – Excitement and Growth in the Human Personality* (Perls, Hefferline, & Goodman, 1973) might be somewhat inaccessible, and that parts of the more recent gestalt literature have been characterised by a certain amount of professional jargon. That might have caused new gestalt therapists to minimise their reading of gestalt literature and led outsiders to give up on the literature before grasping the full depth and range of the approach. Similarly, few gestalt practitioners have been associated with university environments, which means that formal studies into the effects of gestalt therapy have been far rarer than studies of, for example, the more cognitive and behavioural approaches. As a consequence, many have misunderstood what the gestalt approach is really about.

It is widely known that Perls was a master of developing techniques for triggering therapeutic processes and of making highly compelling presentations of these techniques in workshops and video performances. Some (e.g., Kellogg, 2014) have found qualified inspiration in this towards integrating gestalt methods with cognitive schema therapy. Others, however, have erroneously concluded that the essence of the gestalt approach lies purely in techniques, and that

practising gestalt therapy is about mastering the technical approach—
for example, the two-chair technique. Further, many of Perls' famous
sayings have been taken a little too literally. For example, what may
be his best-known statement: "lose your mind and come to your
senses", has led some to view the gestalt approach as a catharsis therapy, which is exclusively about connecting with, and expressing, one's
emotions. Similarly, the so-called "gestalt prayer", "I do my thing, and
you do your thing . . . if by chance we find each other it's beautiful. If
not, it can't be helped" (Perls, 1969), which points out that the existential meeting of individuals cannot be forced, has been used to
justify uninhibited and transgressive behaviour that shows no concern
for others.

There is a name for this aspect of the gestalt approach, which
many have encountered in this manner and which they came to
see as its essence: It is Perls-ism (Clarkson & Mackewn, 1993). It uses
a great deal of jargon, and it has done nothing good for the reputa-
tion of the gestalt approach. It has fuelled the perception that gestalt
work is simply a set of techniques and primarily a highly confron-
tational therapy approach that revolves around experiencing and
catharsis.

To some extent, Perls-ism has overshadowed Perls' true genius.
Fritz Perls (in cooperation with his wife, Laura Perls) was brilliant at
taking important fundamental principles and core insights from various philosophical, psychological, neurological, and spiritual positions
and integrating them creatively into a coherent approach. He also
excelled in his use of creative experimentation and was able to engage
people's phenomenology in new ways that made it possible to work
in the here and now with the structural patterns that make it difficult
for them to lead full and satisfying lives. The outcome of these efforts
deserves to be taken seriously, and that is indeed one of the primary
aims of this book.

With regard to our ambition, we are aware of the objections that
have been raised against the gestalt approach for having a weak
theoretical structure and, in particular, for lacking a more specific
theory of development. These objections are valid in the sense that, on
a theoretical level, the gestalt approach has a very minimalist core
structure, as it has not involved efforts to create sophisticated structural models of the psyche and its development. The core theoretical
underpinning of the approach is a set of fundamental principles for

the way in which the human organism relates to its environment. That creates a conceptual framework for exploring and understanding the human phenomenology, as it unfolds in the here-and-now situations where one encounters it. As a positive feature, this encourages a consistently process-orientated approach to the human life processes that are addressed in therapy. It is a virtually empty conceptual framework that is open to embracing and integrating insights and acquired knowledge from other theoretical and practical approaches. It is true, as one objection goes, that a drawback of this openness is that it gives the individual gestalt therapist a great deal of latitude (perhaps too much) for deciding what to put into this framework and, thus, how to practise gestalt therapy. In our opinion, however, the response to this should not be to produce fixed models and manuals that restrict our ability to understand and address the complexity of human life processes. Instead, the response should be to be even more explicit about the fundamental principles that are at play in these life processes, and how they can be applied in practical gestalt work.

On this basis, our intention with this book is to demonstrate the implications of a new integrative gestalt practice in both theory and practice. Our choice of the term *integrative* gestalt practice (IGP) underscores the integrative ambition of providing a framework that is capable of integrating other theoretical approaches with an approach that, in itself, by virtue of its field orientation, integrates bodily, cognitive, psychodynamic, motivational, and systemic understandings and interventions. In regard to this ambition, we have found essential inspiration in Wilber's (1995, 2000, 2006) integral–holistic approach, which we will seek to integrate with the fundamental gestalt theory concepts about field, organism, and the gestalt formation process.

Further, by calling it integrative gestalt *practice*, we aim to signal that the approach goes beyond the narrowly defined therapeutic setting. This is not merely a therapeutic approach but an approach to working with human life processes in (virtually speaking) any context. Hence, throughout the book, we use the terms *IGP practitioner* and *person* rather than therapist and client in discussing the practical IGP work in various contexts. In some cases, we have found it more appropriate to use the terms therapist and client, but these will be exceptions from the core message of IGP, which is that it is a general approach to human work in any genre where one works with people: in treatment, education, supervision, counselling, etc.

Reader's guide

We set out by outlining the fundamental understanding and the key concepts of IGP. These aspects are addressed in Chapters One–Three, which present and discuss the concepts of the field, the organism, and the gestalt formation process (in that order) as they are understood in the IGP approach. Further, Chapter Four will demonstrate how awareness, contact, and experimentation serve as key components on the path from the theoretical conceptual understanding to the practical IGP work. Next, Chapter Five will provide examples of how the IGP approach can be applied in relation to various practical life and work conditions. In Chapter Six, we discuss the broader perspectives of the IGP approach and its applicability as a basis for integrating different approaches to working with individuals and systems, and we discuss how IGP can provide holistic perspectives on health, disease, and politics.

In Appendix I, we offer some additional proposals to supplement the training exercises that we use in our IGP training, including IGP awareness training (which is an advanced type of awareness exercise akin to mindfulness). In Appendix II, we point to the research methodological consequences of IGP by presenting Wilber's integral methodological pluralism.

Throughout the book, you will encounter three types of boxes: reflection boxes, definition boxes, and exercise boxes. Reflection boxes elaborate on a point or offer reflections in relation to the main text. Definition boxes specify definitions of the concepts that are introduced in the chapters. Exercise boxes describe practical exercises related to the main text with the purpose of enhancing experiential and integrated learning.

We hope that you will experience just some of the excitement stemming from thinking in terms of complexity and wholeness that has characterised our writing process, and we hope that you will enjoy biting into, chewing on, and digesting the text.

Prelude: complexity and perspective taking

It is a fundamental assumption in IGP that people's knowledge of
what we call reality involves construction. Although human perception allows us to see aspects of our environment as they are (for
example, that a seagull flies), our perception of what we see is associated with a considerable amount of "mind stuff" that contributes to
the meaning we perceive when we see what we see. When we see
something in our environment (for example, a flying seagull), we see
it as a figure within a much larger amount of information and sensory
data that also affect our mind and our consciousness. Most of the
sensory impressions that we are exposed to along with what we see
affect us on a much more subtle level outside of our awareness.

In itself, our tendency to perceive in meaningful wholes causes us
to fragment reality. In our way of ascribing meaning to reality, we
break the coherent field into distinct units or dualities such as organism–environment, psyche–soma, figure–ground. Thus, dualism
becomes a part of our general way of thinking.

In our efforts to preserve the role of complexity and the complementarity of dualities in the field without being trapped in a dualist
way of thinking, as IGP practitioners, we rely on a systematic field
model that considers every gestalt or whole from four fundamental
perspectives: a singular and a plural perspective and an interior and
an exterior perspective. Thus, in relation to human life processes, we
pay equal attention to the individual's interior phenomenological
perspective (thoughts and emotions) and to what we can observe from
the outside with regard to the individual's behaviour and physiology.
Similarly, we pay equal attention to interior and exterior aspects of
the individual's environment, which consists of interactions among
people, system structures and system functions (in the exterior perspective) and of shared meaning making and culture (in the interior
perspective). The four quadrants in the model below represent these
four basic perspectives on human life processes. A chair in each corner
marks the four perspectives (Figure 1).

The theoretical and practical applications of this field-orientated
perspective model, which is based on Ken Wilber's work, will be
unfolded in more detail. It is essential to the IGP approach and forms
a recurring theme in the book.

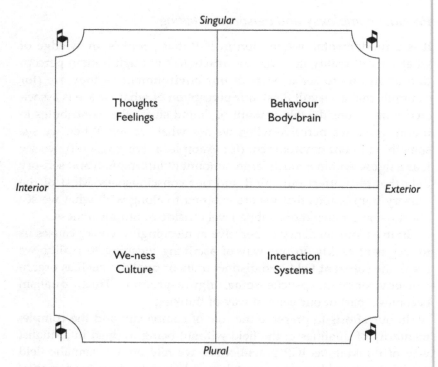

Figure 1.   The four basic perspectives on human life processes.
A variation of Ken Wilber's quadrant model.

CHAPTER ONE

The field

The integrative gestalt approach is holistic and field-orientated. The intention of this is to avoid reducing one's understanding of the whole person with whom one is working to a set of personality traits, a set of cognitive schemas, a psychic apparatus, a particular diagnosis, or similar reductions. The problem with such reductions is that the specific knowledge they have to offer about their limited area of focus usually fails to paint a very good picture of the complex context that this limited knowledge is embedded in. A holistic, field-based understanding means working with "the whole person".

Holism: the whole is more than the sum of its parts

The word holism comes from Greek (holos) and means whole. As a philosophy, holism aims to view phenomena as wholes rather than as combinations of parts. The point of this holistic understanding is that *the whole is more than the sum of its parts*, and that it does not, therefore, make sense to reduce a whole to its constituent parts if it is the whole one wishes to understand. That the whole is more than the sum of its parts is exactly what characterises a gestalt (for example, a musical stanza); a gestalt constitutes a whole that cannot be broken down into its constituent parts without loss of meaning and function. In the traditional gestalt approach, the holistic inspiration can be traced back to the neurologist Kurt Goldstein, experimental perceptual psychology, Eastern philosophy (particularly Perls' experiences with Zen Buddhism in Japan) and Jan Smuts' (1926) holistic thinking. The holistic perspective should be seen in relation to the field concept. The field concept in the gestalt approach has its roots in natural science, which is where Kurt Lewin (1952) acquired it, from the studies of electromagnetic fields and time in the framework of relativity theory. In that sense, the gestalt approach with its holistic structure and field concept reflects a meeting of Eastern and Western complexity of thinking.

In IGP we structure and systematise our understanding of holism by applying a particular field theoretical approach to the gestalt formation process. This approach is based on the so-called holon concept and holarchical understanding as applied by Ken Wilber (1995). Let us first take a closer look at the holon concept before explaining the field concept.

A holarchy is a hierarchy, but not just any hierarchy. A holarchy is a holistic hierarchy that includes and organises the wholes that it consists of and relates to. The concept of the holarchy is based on the concept of the holon, which, as in the gestalt approach, implies that phenomena in the world should be understood as wholes (holons), each of them a whole in itself but also part of a larger whole. Thus, for example, atoms both exist in themselves and are part of molecules, which in turn similarly exist in themselves and are parts of cells, which in turn exist in themselves and are part of organs, which in turn exist in themselves and are part of organisms, which in turn exist in themselves as *individual holons* and are part of *social holons* in the form of groups, organised in eco-niches, cultures, societies, etc. Transferring this concept to human behaviour, we similarly find that a certain type of behaviour in a person constitutes a whole that is part of a larger whole, which contains a multiplicity of historical and contextual aspects. In a holarchical perspective, the focus will be on understanding how here-and-now behaviour might relate to a similar type of behavioural functionality at an earlier time in the person's life. For example, that the current type of behaviour was formed as a holon during the person's childhood based on the understanding of the circumstances that the person was capable of at the time.

According to the holon concept, to understand the individual phenomenon (the individual gestalt or holon) one should seek to understand it both in its characteristic individual quality and in its connections to the larger wholes of which the phenomenon is a part. This may be understood both in an immediate horizontal dimension and in a vertical dimension.

In the horizontal dimension, we find all the things that a phenomenon is directly connected to at any given time. In the vertical dimension, we find the larger contexts that the individual phenomena are part of, and which they are organised within. It is in the vertical dimension that we discover the meaning of the person's values, that is, how they are manifested, and how they affect and shape the person's direction in life.

EXAMPLE

Using our project of writing this book as an example, in the horizontal dimension, we find the computer we are currently typing on or the concrete configurations of how we sit in relation to each other while we type, and what we discuss with each other. In the vertical dimension, we find the larger contexts that this writing project is part of and that it is organised within. This involves the very idea of writing a book together, which makes us coordinate our actions and adjust our mutual contributions to each other based on what the idea of the writing project requires of each of us.

With its holarchical structure, the holon concept overcomes the problem of the versions of holistic thinking which claim that relations are arbitrary, and that everything is, therefore, *merely* relative. This arbitrary understanding of holism misses the key point that holons are hierarchically organised in the sense that higher-level holons transcend and include lower ones. When holons thus organise hierarchically, the result is an *inclusive hierarchy*, where the individual hierarchy is both something in itself and also part of other hierarchical organisations—just as we view the individual gestalt as a whole in itself, but also as part of a larger, that is, a more inclusive, gestalt. These hierarchies, which include lower hierarchies that they have in turn transcended, are called *holarchies*. Thus, the holarchy is a hierarchical structure that includes all the wholes that have gone into creating it. At the same time, the holarchy relates to other holarchically ordered wholes, and together with these it enters into a larger structured, holistic whole.

The point is that there is a system to the wholes that we seek to explore in IGP in a holistic framework. These systems reflect holarchical structures that can and will change over time, but which are not, therefore, merely relative and completely arbitrary at any given time. They may be viewed as sorts of *morphogenetic fields* (Sheldrake, 1989): that is, kinds of probability fields where a particular event may be expected to occur, although this cannot be predicted with 100% certainty. In parallel to this point, we speak, in IGP, of *patterns* of organisation and of gestalt inclination, which means that the individual organism has a typical *inclination* for forming certain individually shaped gestalts. This inclination develops as a characteristic adaptation out of both individual constitutional (e.g., genetic) and contextual (e.g., childhood) conditions.

EXAMPLE

If, during his upbringing, a child is often asked by his mother, "Why are you hitting your baby sister?" instead of being told, "I want you to stop hitting your baby sister", the child might develop a certain sensitivity or inclination (based on his or her expectations) later in life to perceive questions as a form of implicit criticism. The person will be prone to this perception, albeit not 100% of the time.

We shall come back to the question of how the organism creates gestalts as a result of the interaction between its gestalt inclination and the field contexts in which the gestalt formation takes place. In the following, we will take a closer look at the field concept and at some of its related aspects and discussions.

The field: an emergent, self-organising totality

In the broadest sense of the word, the field can be said to involve everything that exists and everything that has the potential to exist in the past, present, and future. The field also consists of the mutual relatedness and interactions of all its aspects. The field is in constant motion and change. It exists over time with roots in the past and future-directed horizons of possibilities. In its most abstract form, the field may, in accordance with these characteristics, be defined as *an emergent, self-organising totality.*

This understanding of the field as an emergent, self-organising totality implies the existence of a tendency towards self-organisation in the mutual relations of the field. To illustrate this point, the resulting field organisation can be seen, metaphorically speaking, as a brook finding its natural course in interaction with other natural landscape features. The course of a brook is determined by gravity as well as by the physical conditions in the form of valleys, rocks, etc. that it encounters on its path. The brook takes form in interaction with these field factors. In turn, the brook also shapes the landscape. The brook and the landscape are subject to concrete laws of nature, which determine the conditions by which the landscape shapes the course of the brook, and the brook co-creates the structure of the landscape in a continuous exchange of influences. The course of the brook is a function of interacting elements.

Sticking to the metaphor of the brook, if we imagine that the course of the brook poses a problem, it follows that any access to solving "the problem" or understanding what is perceived as a dysfunction lies in the self-organising nature of the field, which includes both the brook and the landscape. Similarly, one might say that any perceived problem, when seen in a field perspective, contains a set of inherent potential solutions in the sense that the problem is connected with the perceptual perspective from which it is perceived as being a problem. When viewed in a field perspective, something that appears as a problem in a specific perspective will often be found to have both a function and a meaning in relation to the field's way of organising itself. Understanding this function and meaning often reframes what was originally perceived as a problem. In this new light, it may no longer be seen as a problem, which means that the problem has been dissolved as problem. Typically, understanding the field context of a problem also provides access to solutions to the problem. Thus, in a sense, each problem contains a set of possible solutions. Let us look at an example from the area of therapy.

EXAMPLE

Family therapy essentially addresses the family as a whole. In other words, the family is viewed as a system or a "field" where the family members' interactions and behaviour are understood, in part, in light of the whole. In family therapy, uncovering the family system—for example, by means of circular and appreciative enquiry techniques—might reveal that there are issues at play in completely different sections of the system, perhaps in the form of unresolved conflicts between the parents, from which stomach symptoms in their child serve to divert attention, so that the symptoms contribute to preserving a form of homoeostasis in the family system. By uncovering these field relations, the therapy paves the way for a possible solution to the problem.

In extension of the concept of the holarchy, the family, as part of the field, may also be seen as a social holon that is part of more inclusive social holons (the extended family and its genealogical history, the local community, and the larger surrounding society). The family itself also constitutes a holarchy, which includes the family members as holons. One aspect of the holarchical order, for example, is that the parents have experiences with the world that the children lack, and that, unlike the children, they have a responsibility as parents. These factors imply the appreciation of qualitative (and vertical) differences between the "parents-holon" and the "children-holon" and, thus, an openness to understanding how these enter, in a holarchical sense, into the higher-level holon of the "family".

The field is self-organising and contains a holarchical order. This order develops over time, and, thus, the field also has a historical dimension. Therefore, working with the field involves the need to be aware of the dynamics between what we call the "here and now" and the "there and then". The point is that what exists "here and now" carries dimensions of meaning from the past ("there and then") from which it emerges as figure. Thus, it is not only the figure–ground formation that emerges in the present which is interesting, but, rather, the relationship between this figure–ground formation and the more extensive background from which it is forming. The current figure–ground relationship may serve as the focal point of one's investigation, but this figure–ground relationship may also be understood, in itself, as a figure of a particular type of (historically determined) gestalt inclination in the person.

We discuss the role of memory in gestalt inclination in Chapter Two. A further expansion on the gestalt concept is offered in Chapter Three. The historical dimension of the field is discussed later in the present chapter.

REFLECTION BOX 1

Reflections on the field concept

Although the field, in its broadest sense, involves everything: the universe and the interrelatedness of everything, it is also a concept that is used in different ways within different disciplines (physics, mathematics, psychology) to describe the presence within the domain of the individual discipline of interacting relations with the field domain, which should be incorporated into the understanding of the specific objects that are being studied.

There is no single exhaustive field theory, and, thus, although everything is, in principle, interrelated, we do not have one coherent understanding of the nature of everything and its true interrelatedness. Perhaps it would not be possible to arrive at such an understanding.

From a sociological point of view, however, there is generally a growing human awareness of mutual global interrelations, which may be seen as reflecting growing field awareness. In recent years, this field awareness has been promoted by information technology and computer science, climate research (the acknowledgement of ecological regularities and conditions for life), and the globalisation perspective (our mutual relatedness—not least via the Internet). An example of the latter is the experiences with the consequences of a dozen cartoons of a prophet in a Danish newspaper in a larger field context. In fact, we have never before had access to such a vast amount of factual knowledge, experiences, and points of view from so many (often complementary or contradictory) traditions and perspectives as in the past 10–20 years. This requires a growing understanding of how to handle this complexity and how to use this knowledge constructively.

This is a challenge in relation to the inclinations towards predominantly linear, causal, and dualist thinking, which limits our contact with the complexity of reality. Here lies a challenge for mankind in honing our capacity for managing (differentiating and integrating) higher degrees of complexity.

The psychological field vs. the whole field

There is an ongoing discussion in gestalt circles as to whether the field concept in gestalt therapy should be understood as referring exclusively to the psychological field (Staemmler, 2006) or whether it should be seen to include the field in a broader sense, including, but not restricted to, the psychological dimension. The psychological field corresponds to the part of the total field that Lewin (1951) called the person's "life space": those elements of the field that exists in the person's phenomenology. Proponents of the idea that gestalt therapy should only address the psychological field argue that the only thing that exists as reality to, respectively, the client and the therapist, is what they *perceive* as being real, and that it is, therefore, this, respectively shared and subjective, phenomenology that can be defined as the field that is addressed in therapy. In relation to this point, one may speak of the "phenomenal" field, and, as suggested by Staemmler (2006), in this respect, the field may be defined as the intersubjective (or joint) situation that is constituted by the meeting between therapist and client.

If, on the other hand, one has the view that the work concerns the field as a whole, this requires particular awareness to determine when one is dealing with the phenomenological dimension, and when and how one is addressing field dimensions that exist independent of the individual's phenomenological experience. Acknowledging the relevance of an objective reality in therapeutic work implies a risk of seducing (or "pushing") the client to introject the therapist's phenomenological reality as being more (objectively) true than the client's own (Yontef & Jacobs, 2008). This might hamper therapeutic progress, and the therapist must, therefore, be particularly careful to acknowledge the client's phenomenology. In practical IGP work, the psychological field in this regard occupies a particularly crucial role, but it is not the only aspect that is addressed. In our opinion, in both theoretical and practical terms, it hampers the process more than it facilitates it to work exclusively with the field in the meaning of the psychological field than with the field in its totality.

The theoretical limitation in restricting the field concept to the phenomenological (perceived) field is that it produces an unnecessary dichotomy between psychology and other social sciences and the natural sciences, including neuroscience. Sociological studies, for example, uncover systems conditions with a concrete impact on people's lives that are important regardless of whether or not people consider these conditions part of their psychological field. In addition, neuroscience is uncovering neurological factors that condition human phenomenology, regardless of whether or not these people perceive them.

With its holistic field concept, the IGP approach characteristically maintains the option of engaging in dialogue with these (sociological and neurological, etc.) scientific areas regarding the influence of the total field on human life processes.

The practical limitation in restricting the field concept to the psychological field is that it risks overlooking objectively meaningful conditions and factors that exist outside the experiential horizon of the individual person (client). The myriad influences that we are exposed to as human beings, both from our own organism and from our environment, contain a complexity that resides only to a lesser degree in our consciousness and becomes experiences in our phenomenological sphere. In IGP, the goal is to remain open to including all these influential factors in a field concept that embraces both the psychological and the non-psychological parts of the field.

REFLECTION BOX 2

The psychological field vs. the whole field

Staemmler and others advocate an approach that deals exclusively with the psychological field. Such a stance might be motivated for example by a distinction between the concepts of person and organism, where the person (as a phenomenological being) relates to environments with experiential meaning, while the organism (as a biological body) relates to surroundings without experiential meanings. In that case, it is the person in relation to the experiential environment that constitutes the (psychological) field to be addressed, while the organism (the biological body) in relation to its surroundings is not included in the practical field concept. Staemmler (2006, p. 70) uses the schematic presentation below to illustrate the two understandings in relation to one another.

Psychological field or "life space"	non-psychological
person/environment	organism/surroundings

In IGP, we find that a separation of organism and person perpetuates the dualist perception of body and psyche that Perls sought to eliminate, and which is similarly rejected in organismic phenomenology (Merleau-Ponty, 1962). Rather than distinguishing between organism and person, we join Merleau-Ponty in distinguishing between the body as mere physical body and as lived body. The physical body relates to the biological functions of the organism, while the lived body

(continued)

---

relates to the phenomenological intentionality of the organism. Thus, we propose that we cannot understand the functionality of the physical body in its normal mode without considering the embedded intentionality from the lived body as the meaning of the body functionality. Further, it means that we cannot grasp the phenomenological intentionality of the lived body in its normal mode without understanding it as a realisation of the functionality of the physical body. We relate this perspective on the duality of the organism as physical body and lived body to a concept of the field that includes both the psychological and the non-psychological aspects in the environment of the organism. While the concept of the organism includes both a subjective side (the lived body) and an objective side (the physical body), the field concept in IGP also includes both the intersubjective (environmental) and the interobjective (surrounding-related) conditions for the life realisation of the organism. This corresponds to a full quadrant perspective on the organism–environment field.

"Of the field" and "in the field"

A person always relates to something or someone in his or her environment that he/she interacts with and depends on. In the gestalt literature, this is often treated as if there is, on the one hand, an organism and, on the other hand, an environment within which the organism acts. The point is, however, that both organism and environment are aspects of the totality of the whole field. The organism and its environment are not only *in* the organism–environment field. Both are also *of* the field.

The term "*of* the field" means that everything fundamentally exists in a state of interrelatedness where the borders between entities have been eliminated, and out of which something crystallises that we may perceive as entities. In extension of Martin Heidegger's (1962) distinction between being (in a more profound sense of shared being) and beings (as entities in the field), we may say that everything is, from a basic point of view, "*of* the field", but, at the same time, our perception, understanding, and intervention in relation to everything that is "*of* the field" may be at a level where we view it similarly as entities that exist *in* the field, and which, by virtue of their definition as entities, are connected in contact and interaction in a partial section of the field. Thus, although one may view individual organisms as distinct entities, they are always individual entities that are defined by their field-ness (that is, defined by being *of* the field) and which are in contact with other aspects and other beings in field relations (within and with their being *in* the field). On the one hand, it does not make sense to speak of individual organisms as isolated from, and independent of, the field out of which their individuality is constituted. On the other hand, however, we also cannot grasp the character of their individuality unless we maintain that they are *also* distinct entities. Although everything is, in a more profound sense, "of the field", we must also, in practice, address how entities within the field—for example, individuals—interact in a concrete sense. Thus, one might say that everything is "of the field" and interacts "in the field".

In IGP we maintain both perspectives: one perspective states that any element (for example, the individual human being) is part of the larger whole (*of* the field), which also implies that any impact or change in one area also affects other areas of the field; the second perspective states that, at the same time, the individual element in the field interacts as an independent entity with other elements (*in* the field).

Methodological reduction of the field

When applying a field theory approach, in research or in practical work, it is necessary to restrict one's attention in relation to *which part of the field* one is focusing on (Lewin, cited in Perls, Hefferline, & Goodman, 1973, p. 277). Although everything is, in principle, connected on the deeper level of being, and everything, in this sense, is part of the larger field, of course one cannot, in practice, attend, investigate, and intervene in relation to the interactions of everything.

In IGP, we distinguish between the ontological level (of being), where we can consider that everything is connected, and the epistemological level (of knowing), where we need to distinguish between things in order to understand them as entities (although they are, ontologically speaking, interrelated). In practical IGP work, this limitation at the epistemological level takes the form of so-called methodological reductions, where one deliberately includes certain aspects in one's analysis while excluding other aspects. When methodological reductions are done consciously, one will be aware that one's discoveries in connection with the methodological reductions can only constitute partial knowledge in relation to the whole that has been methodologically reduced. This makes it possible to avoid confusing partial knowledge with full-scale knowledge of the whole. Confusing partial knowledge with knowledge of the whole leads to ontological reductionism. By avoiding confusing one's partial knowledge with knowledge of the whole, one can apply methodological reduction while remaining essentially non-reductionist at an ontological level (the endlessly larger whole that constitutes reality). Thus, the point is that methodological reductions can involve a more or less explicit and pronounced awareness of what is captured and what is not captured in one's investigations, and that both the researcher and the practitioner should remain humble with regard to the potential meaning of the aspects that have been left out.

EXAMPLE

An IGP practitioner working one-on-one with a person may include the influence that others in the person's field, for example the person's partner, parents, family background etc., have on the person's situation while also in practice reducing the field to working one-on-one with the person rather than inviting the partner or family to take part in the process. The practitioner should remain aware that it is only the person's phenomenology in relation to these other field aspects that is present in the room. The person's family members may for example have very different perceptions of the phenomenon that the person is presenting.

To ensure a systematic approach to the inclusive concept of the field, as mentioned earlier, IGP draws on inspiration from Ken Wilber's "integral perspectivism". This is also used in training one's capacity for perceiving the complexity of the figure–ground formation process in the field contexts where it unfolds and in addressing multiple dimensions and aspects of the total field simultaneously. The following addresses this field perspective model.

The systematised field model

For a number of years, Wilber (1995, 2000, 2006) has worked to systematise knowledge insights from a variety of areas. In his book *Sex, Ecology, Spirituality* (1995), he introduced the basis of the conceptual model that would later be named the "AQAL model". AQAL stands for all quadrants, all levels. In fact, the AQAL model includes three additional areas: lines of development (all lines), states (all states), and types (all types).

In the following, we take a closer look at the quadrants from the AQAL model and demonstrate how they can be used to systematise the field in an effort to develop the field concept into a more direct and applicable element in IGP work. As the model incorporates the four quadrant perspectives, we will (in accordance with Wilber) refer to it as the *quadrant model*.

As illustrated in Figure 2, the four quadrants represent four different perspectives. The four perspectives represent a distinction

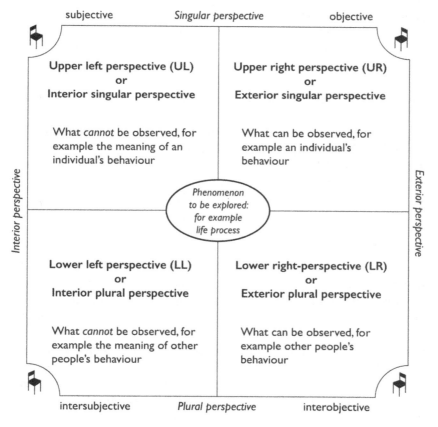

Figure 2.   The quadrant model.

between interior and exterior aspects of things as they are seen, respectively, from a singular and a plural perspective. This produces two *observation perspectives* (the exterior aspects of things as they appear in a singular and a plural perspective) and two *interpretation perspectives* (the interior aspects of things as they appear from a singular and a plural perspective).

What characterises the two observation perspectives is that we can *see* what is happening and what exists, whereas the two interpretation perspectives are characterised by the fact that we cannot immediately see what is happening and what exists. Hence, we have to rely on phenomenological curiosity and interpretation in an attempt to uncover it. For example, if you work as a therapist, you must remain curious and rely on your empathy and interpretation to uncover the phenomenology of the client.

The four perspectives are always present as potential partial perspectives on the totality of a given situation or in relation to a given phenomenon.

- The two upper quadrants capture the *singular dimension* of the phenomenon.
- The two lower quadrants capture the phenomenon in relation to other phenomena—in a *plural dimension*
- The right-side quadrants capture the *exterior* of the phenomenon—the aspects that are accessible to observation.
- The left-side quadrants capture the *interior* of the phenomenon—the aspects that we may learn about by means of an interpretive perspective.

In IGP, we use the quadrant model to address the person's life management from the four basic perspectives. An IGP practitioner working with someone, whether in therapy, supervision, training, or any other context, will operate with a field awareness that can be differentiated into these four perspectives. In accordance with the shape of the quadrant model, the four basic perspectives may be labelled, respectively, upper-right perspective (UR), upper-left perspective (UL), lower-right perspective (LR) or lower-left perspective (LL). They may also be labelled in accordance with the indicated domain: exterior singular, interior singular, exterior plural, or interior plural perspective. It is not that either of these terminologies is better than the other. Both are useful, depending on whether one wants to focus either on the location of one's topic in the model (UR, UL, LR, LL), or on which aspect of a phenomenon is being addressed. Throughout the book, we will be using both sets of labels, but predominantly UR, UL, LR, and LL.

Upper-right quadrant (UR)

The upper quadrants contain perspectives on an individual level. The upper-right quadrant frames the perspective for individual behaviour and for the biological constitution that correlates with the individual's experiences, thinking, and emotions. In this area of the quadrant model, we find the material and physical part of the "self" in a third-person perspective. This includes the physical–biological body and neurophysiological structures and processes, as well as the person's actions and behaviour. This perspective captures observable (exterior) aspects of an individual level. More subtle bodily processes also belong in this quadrant perspective. Although neurobiological processes, for example, are not immediately observable, they can still be made the object of objective observation, given the right equipment. This perspective includes observation of the physical body's living and dying.

Upper-left quadrant (UL)

The upper-left quadrant frames the perspective on the person's thoughts, feelings, and experiences, also known as the person's phenomenology. This perspective includes the person's immediate perceptions, thoughts, and feelings as well as what constitutes the person's mental organisation and self-concept.

This is the area pertaining to our normal concept of consciousness, that is, our "I-ness" in a first-person perspective, which includes an individual's way of producing understanding and meaning. This is the interior singular perspective.

Lower-right quadrant (LR)

The lower-right perspective contains what we can observe in the plural dimension. This is what a video camera will be able to capture when the person moves and interacts with other people in the context that he or she is part of, including exterior objective conditions that the person is not necessarily aware of. It is also in this perspective that we find the rules, laws, systems, and structures, in a narrow as well as a broad sense, that apply in the field that the person is a part of.

We co-exist and interact with other people in a world consisting of a variety of social structures, each with their specific laws, rules, institutions, forms of government, and economic systems: for example, the market economy. Nature, climate, and ecology also co-condition how we organise and how certain aspects of our existence are framed. We interact with each other within all these systems, structures, and contexts, from the broadest to the most intimate. This segment of the field is captured in the lower-right, exterior plural perspective.

Lower-left quadrant (LL)

The *meaning* of what we can observe in the lower-right perspective is created in the lower-left perspective. It pertains to the "interior side" of this "exterior" reality. This is where we find shared meaning and what shapes our *culture*. When we observe, in the lower-right perspective, a group of people running around on a lawn kicking a ball around and are able to notice that they adhere to certain structures and rules, it is from the lower-left perspective that we are able to relate it to their shared understanding of playing football.

The lower-left quadrant is the area for creating a sense of "we-ness", the shared meaning, understanding, and story-telling that lay the foundation for norms, values, and habits and what we generally (on the level of society and organisations) refer to as "culture". When we observe a certain act in the lower-right perspective (for example, a father spanking his child), this may also be uncovered, in a lower-left perspective, as a meaning between the two that relates to their mutual interaction. That is the case even if the father's understanding differs from the child's. For example, the father's meaning might be that he is socialising his child into a desired behaviour, while the child's experience is one of humiliation, suppressed anger, and shame (a feeling that he is not all right). When we examine the thoughts and feelings that accompany and underlie the child's and the father's respective individual experiences, we are back in the upper-left perspective. And when we observe *either* the father spanking the child *or* the child being spanked, holding his breath, clenching his teeth, and giving up a certain behaviour, we are back in the upper-right perspective.

Other terms that pertain to this interior plural perspective are, for example, atmosphere and "informal leadership", etc.

An illuminating way to understand the quadrant perspective model is to imagine it as a window with four different panes. Looking through one particular pane gives us a specific perspective, but it also lets us glimpse, with our peripheral vision, what lies behind the other panes (perspectives). If, however, we think that we can see all that there is to be seen from only one of the panes, and that, therefore, we do not need more than one of the panes to understand the whole of what we are looking at, we have been captured by what Wilber (2006) calls *quadrant absolutism*. Quadrant absolutism is the tendency to reduce what can be seen through the four different perspectives to what is seen through one's favourite perspective. A behaviourist, who operates with reference to the upper-right quadrant, might think that everything that is needed to understand a person is to understand the response pattern in the person's behaviour. A social construction- ist (Gergen, 1994) who operates mainly with reference to the lower-left quadrant perspective might still be interested in what he can learn from a biologist (upper-right quadrant), but if he is basing his under- standing of the totality of *what is* entirely on the lower-left perspective, he has fallen into radical social constructionist quadrant absolutism. Each of the quadrants may lead to quadrant absolutisms based on different reductionist approaches, whether it is in the form of neuro- logical or evolutionary absolutisms in the upper-right quadrant, of systems absolutism in the lower-right quadrant, of phenomenologi- cal absolutism (extreme idealism) in the upper-left quadrant, or of social constructionist or culturalistic absolutism in the lower-left quadrant.

Figure 3 characterises the four perspectives: the interior and exterior of the individual perspective and the interior and exterior of the environmental perspective. In its totality, the field includes it all.

In principle, the quadrant model offers a simple and practically applicable method for differentiating among four basic perspectives

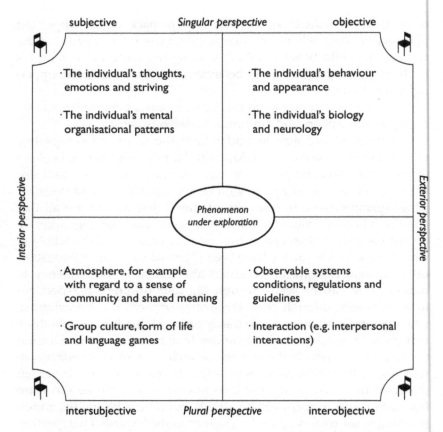

subjective   *Singular perspective*   objective

·The individual's thoughts, emotions and striving

·The individual's mental organisational patterns

·The individual's behaviour and appearance

·The individual's biology and neurology

Interior perspective

Phenomenon under exploration

Exterior perspective

·Atmosphere, for example with regard to a sense of community and shared meaning

·Group culture, form of life and language games

· Observable systems conditions, regulations and guidelines

· Interaction (e.g. interpersonal interactions)

intersubjective   *Plural perspective*   interobjective

Figure 3.   Quadrant observation of the individual in a field context.

on reality. In addition, it offers a means of gaining a higher degree of awareness of the mutual connectedness of the various aspects and their meaning in a field concept. Thus, the model is useful for uncovering how a person's meaning-making processes (in terms of gestalt formations) may be understood as integrations of various differentiations.

To give readers a sense of the specifications of the quadrant model, we include a brief exercise here. The exercise aims to offer a personal experience of the four perspectives and their mutual connectedness that makes it possible to experience the meaningfulness of the model "from the inside".

EXERCISE BOX 1

The exercise should be carried out in a calm and relaxed pace with time to dwell at the individual stages.*

Sit down, get comfortable, and close your eyes.

Upper-left perspective: Direct your attention to your thoughts. Now direct your attention to your feelings. What are you feeling? What are you sensing?

Upper right: Direct your attention to your body. Register your pulse, your heart-beat, and any tension. Now direct your attention to your actions and behaviour. What are you doing, or what are you not doing?

Lower right: Now focus your attention on the contexts you are a part of—in your working life and/or private life. Think of the various people you are in touch with. Also notice which rules, laws, structures, and system contexts you are subject to and part of, for example, in your workplace, the factual hierarchy and the distribution of roles.

Lower left: Now dwell, for example, in the realm of a particular relationship you are a part of, and sense the mood—the atmosphere—and how it might differ from the various other relationships you are a part of.

Upper left: Now return to your perception of the whole—and open your eyes again.

You can find this as an audio-guided exercise at gestalt.dk/exercises.

Looking at *and looking* as

The process described in Exercise Box 1 aims to enhance your understanding of your presence in the quadrant in what Hunt (2009) and Divine (2009) call a *looking as* perspective, that is, your perception of your own presence in the four perspectives as seen from within yourself. The quadrant model may also be used in a *looking at* perspective (Divine, 2009; Hunt, 2009), where you look at yourself from the outside as a person navigating within, and managing, the four quadrants. From this *looking at* perspective, you can aim to understand your own personal capacity for mastering and acting within each of the four quadrants. Similarly, when relating to another person based on the quadrant model, the *looking at* perspective involves looking at the other person's way of mastering their existence in the four quadrants, while the *looking as* perspective involves an attempt at grasping how it feels—*as* the other—to be present in the four quadrant perspectives.

With regard to the *looking at* perspective, the framework of the quadrant model illustrates how the person (whether it is yourself or the other) that you are observing is able *to do* something, more or less competently, within each of the four quadrants.

- In the upper-left quadrant, the focus is on the person's way of managing his or her own thoughts and feelings (the experiential mode), for example, how to remain calm, remain open, and stay in touch with his or her key wishes and goals despite emotional distress and frustration.
- In the upper-right quadrant, the focus is on the person's ability to master his or her action mode, for example, prioritising and achieving activities despite low or failing energy.
- In the lower-right quadrant, the focus is on the person's ability to master a systems and formality mode, for example, mastering technology and navigating in relation to guidelines and formalised requirements from the surroundings.
- In the lower-left quadrant, the focus is on the person's ability to master a relational and reciprocal mode, for example, contributing to the mood and climate in social contexts and managing multiple viewpoints and conflict.

The *looking as* perspective seeks to approximate an interior experience of what it is like to be the person who has experience in the four quadrant perspectives. When working with another person in therapy, for example, one seeks to put oneself in the client's place by focusing on what it must be like *to be* this person with the particular competences and challenges in relation to the tasks, relations, and the self-concept that the person has to relate to. This corresponds to what the classic gestalt literature, with reference to Martin Buber (1937), calls practising "inclusion". Inclusion means that someone, for example the therapist, puts herself in the client's place and from this place also includes a *looking at* perspective on the therapist, that is, on herself. Concepts such as sympathy and empathy also relate to the act of adopting a *looking as* perspective in relation to the other.

- In the upper-left quadrant, the focus is on what it feels like for the person to think, feel, and experience, and to make meaning.
- In the upper-right quadrant, the focus is on what it feels like for the person to act and experience his or her own body and body signals.
- In the lower-right quadrant, the focus is on how it feels for the person to be a part of the systems and relationships that he or she operates within.
- In the lower-left quadrant, the focus is on what it feels like for the person to belong to and be part of a community.

The distinction between the *looking at* and *looking as* perspectives is illustrated in Figure 4, which represents a modified version of Hunt's illustration. In IGP, we view the relationship between *looking at* and *looking as* perspectives as complementary, that is to say, it is possible to adopt either perspective, but once a given perspective becomes figure, the other becomes ground, and *vice versa*. It is, thus, a key aspect of the IGP practitioner's capacity for perspective taking to be able to switch between the *looking at* perspective and the *looking as* perspective, both in relation to oneself and in relation to the people one works with. In Wilber's (2006) terminology, this corresponds to switching between looking at the other in an objectivising quadrivia

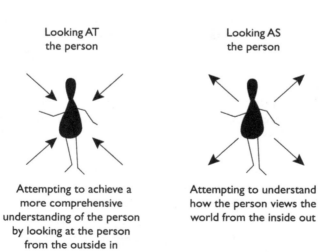

Looking AT
the person

Looking AS
the person

Attempting to achieve a
more comprehensive
understanding of the person
by looking at the person
from the outside in

Attempting to understand
how the person views the
world from the inside out

Figure 4.   *Looking at* and *looking as* perspectives (adapted from Hunt, 2009, p. 79).

(*looking at*) perspective *vs.* looking as the other in a subjectivising empathic quadrant (*looking as*) perspective.

Process and structure in the field

Another complementarity that is addressed in IGP is that of process *vs.* structure. One example of the meaning of this complementarity is found in the concept of self, which includes both structural and process aspects. In a phenomenological sense, the self refers to having a sense of being someone who interacts with something or someone in his or her surroundings and relates to it with intentionality (Hansen, 2001a). The self is both something that exists over time (structure) and something that unfolds at any given moment (process) and is constructed in the given context. When we view the self as *structure*, our focus is on the "enduring characteristics" of the self, as Polster (1995) called it. When we view the self as *process*, our focus is on understanding how a person's experience in any lived moment of being a particular someone relates to the interaction in the contact boundary between organism and environment. In a sense, the perception of the self as *structure* is typical for a *looking at* perspective, while the perception of the self as *process* is typical for a *looking as* perspective.

In Figure 5, the distinction between structure and process is embedded in the four quadrant perspectives. In the figure, the structural aspect is presented in bold, while the processual aspect is shown in italics.

In the *upper-left quadrant perspective*, the focus is on the individual's phenomenology, including the person's thoughts, feelings, and striving. Here, the process aspect should be understood as the perceptions (thoughts, feelings, striving) that exist in the here and now. They are transient and variable: "A moment ago, I was a little sad, but now I am cheerful again." The phenomenological processes reflect the person's specific experience of being who he or she is at any given time. With Wilber (2006), we can call this "the feel of an I", which corresponds exactly to the sense of being present with one's thoughts and feelings as *somebody* who is engaged in doing *something*. In order to understand what this implies, one must adopt a *looking as* perspective.

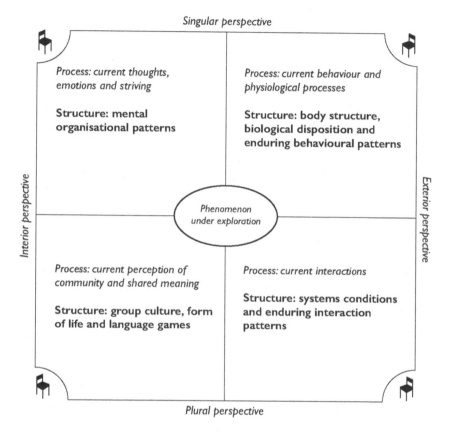

Figure 5. Process and structure in IGP.

The structural aspect, on the other hand, refers to the organisational pattern that forms the basis of what the individual thinks and feels. In everyday speech, this is often referred to as old patterns. Cognitive therapists call it schemata and basic assumptions. Attachment theorists call it working models. With Wilber, we can characterise the structural aspect as "the look of an I", which is to be understood as complementary to the process aspect and the "feel of an I". Herein, "the look of an I" refers to the way or ways in which one, in a *looking at* perspective, makes assumptions (or produces theories) about the individual's organisational dynamics and the developmental state of these organisational dynamics.

Psychology has traditionally offered many different theoretical models concerning "the look of an I"—for example, the psychoanalytic variations on Freud's structural model (1923), Piaget's model of cognitive developmental stages (1937), Loevinger's model of stages of ego development (1976), Kohlberg's (1969) and Fowler's (1981) variations on Piaget's theory of stages of moral development, and Graves' (1970) theory on values and levels of existence. In Wilber's (2000) framework, the structural aspects in the upper-left quadrant are related to how the person might have more or less capacity in various *lines of development* and various *stages* in these lines of development. By focusing on the multiple lines of development, we can bring explicit attention to the developmental balances and imbalances between the different lines. An example of imbalance could be found in a person with highly developed intellect but a less developed moral sense, etc. (see p. 33).

In IGP we are aware of the risk that such structural models degenerate into what Perls called "fixed institutions", but still we find it necessary to apply a theoretical understanding of how the structural aspect of the interior singular quadrant perspective reflects *a particular inclination in the individual to form gestalts in a typical manner.* We call this particular inclination a *procedural gestalt inclination.* This is not a "fixed institution" but, rather, an inclination for forming and resolving gestalts that are embedded in the person's procedural memory and internalised self-regulation. We will explain this point in depth later.

The process aspect of the *upper-right quadrant perspective* is the individual's concrete acts and physiological processes. The structural aspect refers both to enduring behaviour patterns and to somatic symptoms over time. An expression of the structural aspect in this perspective would be, for example, the physical manifestations of the mental organisation pattern, which is reflected, for example, in the person's posture, muscle tone, muscle armour, breathing, etc. Such aspects are addressed by body-orientated approaches (see, e.g., Feldenkrais, 1972; Kepner, 2001; Lowen, 1967; Reich, 1980).

The natural body response to a threatening situation may be to hold one's breath, tense one's shoulders, and turn one's head away to avoid the danger. Such a response may be viewed as a process aspect in the upper-right quadrant perspective. However, if the sense of danger is permanent, this bodily adaptation to the situation may become an organised adaptation *structure* manifested in the body. Within the field of gestalt therapy, James Kepner has focused on this aspect, and he writes,

> . . . Organismic processes of adaptation and adjustment become fixed body structures when they are used habitually—either because the environment constantly requires the same response, or because we come to fix our sense of self, allowing ourselves little flexibility. (Kepner, 2001, p. 49)

When seeing the physiological expression of the structure in the procedural gestalt inclination in the above perspective, the differentiation between *looking as* and *looking at* makes it possible to distinguish between sensing what it is like *to be* this physiological expression from within—for instance, if the practitioner asks the person to *be* his tapping foot as a way of bringing unidentified aspects/feelings to awareness (*looking as*)—and what it is like *to do* what it does, as it appears from the outside (*looking at*).

The process aspect of the *lower-right quadrant perspective*, for example, concerns the interactions that actually occur between people, and which might be captured by a video camera at any given moment. The structural aspect includes the systems and structures that interactions, over time, help to create. The rules and laws of a society stem from the fact that, over time, interpersonal interactions have given rise to mechanisms of control and regulation. Looking at a school, one may observe children and teachers coming, interacting, and going. That would be a process aspect in the exterior plural quadrant perspective. However, even when nobody is present at the school, there is still the school building, equipment, and furnishings, teaching materials, rules of conduct, government guidelines for education, etc. That pertains to the structural aspect in the lower-right quadrant. In this perspective, too, one may distinguish between imagining seeing things from within the system perspective (*looking as*) and viewing the system perspective from without (*looking at*). Among other possibilities, the *looking as* perspective makes it possible to uncover the networks of behaviour over time, which includes interactions and communication among the members of the system. Communication, for example, is the focal point in theories on social autopoiesis (cf. Luhmann, 1995).

The process aspect of the *lower-left quadrant perspective* involves, for example, the current and transient experience of shared meaning that two or more persons can have together. The structural aspect then refers to the organisational principles of shared meaning over time in the form of collective and cultural organisation patterns.

In the same way as with the relation between "the feel of an I" and "the look of an I" in the upper-left quadrant, a distinction can be drawn here between "the feel of a we" and "the look of a we" (Wilber, 2006, pp. 154–156). While "the feel of a we" refers to a multiplicity of individuals' concrete experiences of shared meaning (in the *looking as* perspective), "the look of a we" refers to the organising collective and cultural patterns, with their language games and life forms, that frame the experiences of shared meaning (as they are uncovered in the *looking at* perspective). For example, when we distinguish, in our understanding of cultural differences, between individualist and collectivist cultural patterns (Triandis, 1995), this tells us something about how people growing up under these cultural patterns are affected by certain meaning horizons that influence the way they see each other and themselves (*looking at*). Within these patterns (or among them, for that matter) two (or more) individuals may then have the experience of having a shared understanding of cultural logics that forms the basis of the specific ways in which they experience meaning when they talk with each other (*looking as*).

Exercise Box 2 describes an exercise that might help you get the structural aspects of the quadrant model under your skin. The challenge here is to adopt a *looking at* perspective on your enduring patterns and structures in order to understand their character.

EXERCISE BOX 2

The exercise* should be carried out in a calm and relaxed pace with time to dwell on the individual stages. Sit down, get comfortable, and close your eyes.

Upper-left perspective: Direct your attention to your thoughts as they are at this time in your life—can you discern a pattern in the form of typical thoughts you have about yourself and the world? Now direct your attention to your feelings as they typically are . . . Try to see if you can discern a pattern. Perhaps you can also recognise the patterns from before—the so-called old patterns.

Upper right: Now try to direct your attention to your physical body . . . and pay attention to the structural aspect in the form of, for example, persistent symptoms, your posture, and your breathing. Now turn your attention to your actions

(continued)

and your behaviour. What are you doing, or what do you avoid doing—do you see a pattern?

Lower right: Now direct your attention to the contexts you are a part of. Think of the various people you are in contact with. Think of the system contexts you enter into. Notice whether you recognise typical ways and patterns in your own behaviour in relation to others.

Lower left: Now dwell a little on the contexts and relations you are part of, and sense the mood—"the atmosphere". Also note which recurring patterns you become aware of in your experience and self-perception in these contexts.

You can find this as an audio-guided exercise at gestalt.dk/exercises.

The distinction between process and structure has a parallel in Wilber's (2006) distinction between inside perspectives (process) and outside perspectives (structure) in each of the four quadrants. This produces a total of eight perspectives, or zones, that may form the basis of specifying eight prototypes of research methodology each in their link to the subject area they explore (Wilber, 2006). Wilber's zone system is described in more detail in Appendix II.

The history of the field

With the distinction between structure and process, we can now return to the previously mentioned point that the field has a history (see Figure 6). Structural patterns are created over time and take shape based on what they were before. Thus, they are what they are by virtue of their history. The structures that we find in the field are both something in themselves and something in the sense of being a result of something else that has preceded their emergence. Structures are holarchical, that is, they emerge by both transcending and including what they once were.

This matches the general concept of development in IGP, which says that a holon (or a gestalt) on a higher level transcends and includes holons on lower levels (cf. the section below). Thus, working with the field not only requires a *horizontal* awareness of the field's current structure and process conditions, but also a *vertical* awareness of the influence of the past on the workings of current structures and processes. The key to understanding the meaning of current actions,

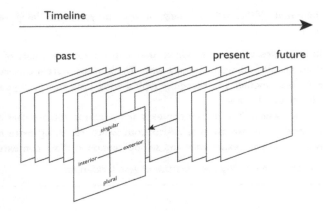

Timeline

past   present   future

Figure 6. The field includes the history of the field.

self-perceptions, and perceptions of one's surroundings is to understand how past and present interact in the present. This applies both
to individual factors (the individual person) and to groups and organisations. For example, a company's previous organisation culture
(lower left) might still show its face in a situation when the company
is under new management or has undergone major organisational
changes (lower right). The current functioning of a group (lower right)
might be governed by a (more or less tacit) saga about what the group
was once like (lower left), even if most of the members are new to the
group. Also, individuals might repeat behaviours (upper right) that
they thought they had left behind, but which continue to occupy a
place in their mental organisation (upper left). The expression "old
habits die hard" refers precisely to the inertia that characterises our
mental organisation when we encounter new situations.

New situations, however, not only activate old habits, but also
contain new opportunities, which contribute to the organising of the
field in the present. The present moment of the current horizontal field
is, in fact, extended vertically between past and future, where the link
between people's behaviour here and now, their past learning, and
their future-orientated life projection is built into the holarchical
developmental dynamics of the field. Each moment inherently contains a potential movement or process *from* something and *towards* a
subsequent something. Even if we cannot know the future in factual
terms, remaining open to the future in all the quadrant perspectives

of the present moment will improve our capacity for sensing the nascent aspects in the ever emerging field (cf. Scharmer, 2007).

Development of and in the field

The theoretical concept of *development* in IGP is associated with the holarchical quality of the holon concept, which, as described earlier, states that a holon (corresponding to a gestalt) on a given level both transcends and includes lower-level holons. It should be noted that this is a structural concept of development that says nothing about the content of what develops but which relates to the character of the organisational structure that a given content enters into on a certain level of development. A holon on a given organisational level contains the qualities that the included holons on lower organisational levels possess individually, but it also—by virtue of the transcendence—contains more and other qualities than lower-level holons. Development refers to the path from a lower to a higher organisation of holons, and, thus, development has occurred once something has transcended a previous level of functioning and subsequently functions on a more complex level of organisation. Thus, and in a formal sense, development can be defined as the emergence of a growing capacity for containing complexity and for differentiating and integrating the content of what develops. With regard to human psychological development, this involves a growing capacity for perspective taking and for embracing a nuanced understanding of oneself and one's surroundings. This growing capacity also reflects an increased perspectival depth (Wilber, 2006), where depth refers to verticality in the holarchical development.

The condition for this development to take place is first to identify *what is*, then to dis-identify from it, and, next, to reintegrate the dis-identified on a higher level of mental organisation. In this context, Kegan (1994) says that what is a subject on one level (that is, what you perceive yourself as) becomes an object for the subject on a higher level.[1] When this has occurred, a development has taken place where you initially identified with being a subject before dis-identifying from being a subject and, thus, becoming an object for the subject on a higher level. To the extent that the new object is related to other objects on the new subject level, it can be reintegrated at this new level: something that you previously perceived yourself as being at one with has now become something that you can relate to as an integrated aspect of what you are.

A cardinal point in the concept of holarchical development is to dis-identify from what calls for being reintegrated on a higher level. To dis-identify from something that concerns yourself (for example, a particular image of yourself or certain feelings), you must first identify with it (from a *looking as* to a *looking at* perspective); that is, you must accept responsibility for this particular self-image or for harbouring these particular feelings. That is impossible if you are unaware of what is going on—if, for example, you are in the grip of (identical with) your feelings. Thus, development proceeds through a state of being *identical with* to (via awareness and contact) *identify as* and, eventually, *dis-identify from*. Unless you identify the feelings and thoughts that *are*, you will not be in a position to have anything from which to dis-identify. In that case, these thoughts and feelings will either go unnoticed, or they will be perceived as something other than they are. For example, someone who had the experience, during the period of growing up, that showing anger was prohibited, might develop a tendency to feel sadness rather than anger, which will prevent the person from ever truly managing to feel and identify the underlying emotion (of anger). Conversely, a person might also have had the experience that it was wrong to show vulnerability and sadness and, therefore, learnt to cover up these emotions by expressing anger instead. In either case, the subsequent development process will be off balance with regard to the affected areas.

You cannot dis-identify from something that you have not identified with. The processes of separating out feelings, thoughts, and perceptions without relating to them and identifying with them are not dis-identification processes, but dissociation processes. When dissociation occurs instead of dis-identification, it blocks the ability to integrate the dissociated material on a higher level of functioning. For example, if a state of shock becomes chronic, the person becomes identical with the state. In that case, the person *is unable to* identify with it via awareness (which implies a *looking at* perspective) and consequently cannot dis-identify from it. The person is unable to see it in a *looking at* perspective. Someone who has undergone, for example, a divorce, and who is unwilling to bring awareness to, and accept, his altered life situation as part of dis-identifying from the image of the person he was before the change will be unable to discover the experiences and the new development that such a dis-identification (which may include anger, grief, forgiveness, and acceptance) would enable.

Generally, development is an ongoing process of comparing your phenomenology (left-quadrant perspectives) with objective reality (right-side quadrants). Bringing awareness to *what is* constitutes the foundation and often the direct trigger of development, while a lack of awareness of *what is* frequently poses the key obstacle to development. This is what is referred to as the "paradoxical theory of change" in the gestalt literature (see Beisser, 1971).

To illustrate, Beisser describes in *Flying Without Wings* (1990, p. 56) how he was infatuated with the image of himself before he was struck down by polio, so much so that he was convinced that his girlfriend similarly could only ever be attracted to young men possessing the healthy body that he once had, even though she had not known him then. Only over time did he learn to accept that what his girlfriend was attracted to, in fact, was not the image he was clinging to, but, instead, who he actually was now, with his disability.

Quadrant development

The developmental processes that we have discussed here do not occur in isolation. Development occurs in all four quadrants, and what happens in one quadrant affects aspects of what happens in the other quadrants. A full understanding of the conditions of the developmental process that takes place in one of the quadrants thus involves consideration of developmental levels, states, and processes in the other quadrants. The diagonal spirals in Figure 7 illustrate the dynamic and complex process of the levels of development in the respective quadrants.

The term *quadrant development* refers to the holistic notion of something new emerging in each of the quadrants when something existing is both transcended and included in the resulting higher level of organisation. The path of quadrant development, as mentioned earlier, goes from elementary to gradually more complex levels of organisation and, thus, increased holarchical depth.

- In the upper-left quadrant, the process might involve, for example, cognitive, emotional, moral, and interpersonal lines of

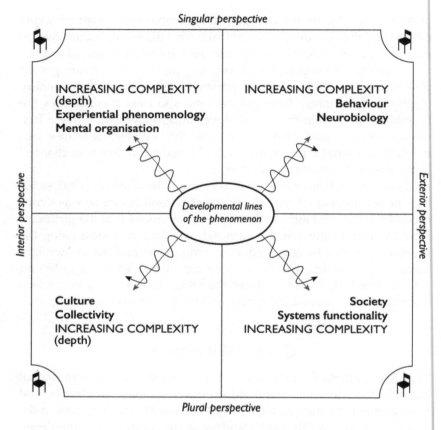

Figure 7. Quadrant development.

development from the most elementary level to increasingly complex levels of mental organisation.

- In the upper-right quadrant, the process might involve, for example, the biological development and behavioural manifestations of organisms and, in the case of human development, phenomena such as constitutional dispositions in the form of traits, temperament, stimulation level, etc. that can be observed objectively. It might also pertain to the evolutionary development of the brain from a reptilian and a mammalian brain to the higher primate brain and the emergence of the neocortex.
- In the lower-left quadrant, the process might involve, for example, the cultural development from pre-modernity through

modernity and post-modernity towards—to use Wilber's term—
integral holism. It might also involve culturally conditioned
discursive frameworks relating to values, meaning, morals, and
linguistic semantics.

- In the lower-right quadrant, the process might involve, for example, various forms of communities and institutions that develop
as a result of changes in production from hunter–gatherer communities through agricultural communities to industrial and
information-technological societies.

Thus, development involves identification, dis-identification, transcendence, and inclusion, in contrast to dissociation, which hampers
development. In the framework of the quadrant model, if we focus,
for example, on organisational development, we can see how a possible initiative in one quadrant perspective that is not matched by development in another quadrant perspective could result in dissociation
rather than development.

EXAMPLE

When an organisation implements organisational changes (lower right),
such as initiatives aimed at strengthening individual competences (upper
quadrants), and these initiatives are later found to have undesirable and
unintended consequences for the organisational culture (lower left), true
development can be achieved if a follow-up analysis results in the integration of the acquired experiences in subsequent initiatives (as this both
integrates and transcends the previous level of development). By contrast,
it would be an expression of dissociation if the initiatives are uncritically
scrapped without any effort to determine what is useful and what is not.

Aspects in other quadrants will affect the understanding of a given
phenomenon in one quadrant but, in addition, within the individual
quadrant one should also be aware of the various lines of development that exist here and of the fact that their development is simultaneously independent and interrelated (Wilber, 2006). For example, the
upper-left quadrant may simultaneously involve a complex organisation in the cognitive line of development as well as an emotional or
moral line of development with a less complex organisation. Thus, it
is possible to be cognitively advanced while having attained a less

advanced emotional or moral level of development (for example, the intelligent psychopath). Particularly pronounced imbalances might be associated with various forms of personality disorders which have poor figure–ground connections, etc., while less pronounced imbalances will be more typical reflections of ordinary complexities in people's life development and their field surroundings.

REFLECTION BOX 3

Existential conditions. As part of the human condition (that is, as part of the history and development of the field), we are all going to die at some point; this might cause fear of death and implies an existential responsibility for creating a meaningful existence before it is too late. In some versions of gestalt thinking, this basic existential condition has been associated with the point of view that philosophical and psychological existentialism is a particular cornerstone in (or underlying) the gestalt approach (Hostrup, 2010).

In IGP, we take the same approach to the basic existential conditions for human life as we do to any other basic issue: that is, we address them in accordance with quadrant logic and the four quadrant perspectives. In this light, the basic existential conditions are reflected in the two exterior perspectives by virtue of the fact that biological life begins and ends at a given time and the fact that it is inevitably manifested in social and institutional system contexts. This frames our approach to the way people respond, cognitively, emotionally, and in the form of ideas and narratives (sometimes of a religious nature), both on an individual (interior singular) and a collective (interior plural) level, including cultural differences.

It is characteristic of existential philosophers that their approach combines the exterior perspective with the interior perspective. The factual conditions of existence (exterior) form the basis of thoughts and feelings that—as existential philosophers point out—may generate a phenomenology characterised by anxiety. The conflict is that we know that we have to die, and that we do not want to die. According to existential philosophers (Kierkegaard, 1965; Sartre, 1948), living one's life with the awareness that one must die means acknowledging and living with existential angst (unlike neurotic anxiety), existential loneliness, and the imperative of choosing (and assuming responsibility for) oneself. In IGP, this right–left complementarity is an underlying and often explicit aspect of the practical work with the individual person. Optimal organismic self-regulation—throughout the life (and death) process—means being responsibly present in accordance with, and influenced by, the circumstances that frame one's existence, independent of whether these circumstances give rise to, for example, joy, pain, anxiety, or helplessness.

Quadrant analysis of stress as an example

The following will illuminate the phenomenon of stress in the light of quadrant logic. The phenomenon of stress is something most people are familiar with to some degree, and it is often regarded as an individual problem that pertains to an individual's failure to manage his or her life situations, typically in relation to work or education. A quadrant approach to the phenomenon will, however, show that it is never sufficient to view stress as a strictly individual issue or, for that matter, as a phenomenon that concerns only one of the quadrants. This is illustrated in Figure 8, where we have placed stress in the

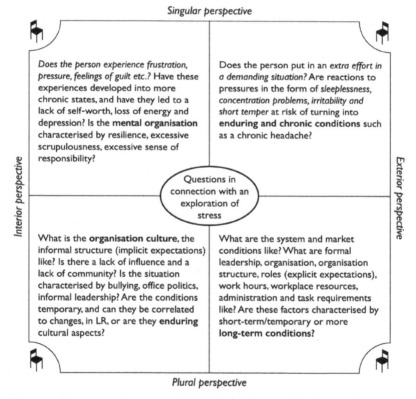

Figure 8. Process and structure: IGP analysis of stress. The figure shows some possible questions in connection with a quadrant exploration of stress and how these questions relate to process and structural aspects, respectively. Process aspects are presented in italics, structural aspects in bold face.

centre of the model. To do so is the typical first step in a quadrant analysis. The next step then typically involves associating the phenomenon with a life situation, which is then unfolded and examined in the four quadrants, paving the way for a summary that will clarify possible connections between the factors conditioning the phenomenon in all four quadrants. Through that, we reach a qualified quadrant base for the subsequent work.

In the present example, a manager contacts the IGP practitioner after having to take sick leave due to severe stress symptoms. For about a year, the manager has been assigned an area of responsibility that involves more departments than before. Conversations with the manager reveal that in the past year he has often felt tired and sad after having to work late nights and weekends. After a holiday or a few days off, he has felt fine again. This we register in the *upper-left quadrant* as a process aspect in a *looking as* perspective. After some time with an increased workload, the manager has experienced a more persistent sense of fatigue with no opportunity to recuperate, which has gradually led to burn-out with symptoms of depression. This has affected his gestalt formation inclination and led to a general loss of focus, lack of concentration, etc. Viewed in a *looking at* perspective, these more permanent aspects of his mental mode register as a structural aspect in the upper-left quadrant perspective. His structurally conditioned inclination to display a high degree of conscientiousness and diligence means that he fails to draw balanced boundaries in accordance with his capacities.

If we look at the stress case in relation to the *upper-right quadrant perspective*, it might be about a transient pressure that temporarily affects the manager's organism—for example, his blood pressure. The structural aspect of this process aspect might, for example, if it continues over time, be expressed in chronically elevated blood pressure, persistent headaches, and other symptoms. This perspective also involves a differentiation between *looking as*, which refers to being the lived body with its factual symptoms, and the *looking at* perspective, which considers the body's way of handling the symptoms.

In the upper-right perspective, the structural aspects from the left (phenomenological) side are correlated with structural aspects of the body, for example, as they are expressed in the manager's posture, muscle armour, breathing, chronic tension, etc. It is likely that there are constitutional factors related to differences in sensitivity, which will influence different people's tendency to develop stress symptoms.

That some people develop symptoms of stress and burn-out while others do not might also be conditioned by the gestalt inclination and the gestalt patterns that individuals—in the upper-left quadrant perspective—bring with them from their upbringing: for example, in form of an inclination to conscientiousness, an excessive sense of responsibility, a drive to excel in order to receive recognition, an inability to draw boundaries and look after oneself, etc. Here, we see the importance of the historical dimension of the field and of the relationship between "here and now" and "there and then".

In the *lower-right quadrant perspective,* in the manager's workplace there may be observable behaviour (in a *looking at* perspective) in the manager's supervisor and colleagues that acts as a stressor. This could involve ambiguous definitions of roles, hierarchies, and mandates, or simply a lack of manpower. When the organisation's system dimension is viewed in a *looking as* perspective, these ambiguities or shortages may be perceived as the result of necessary but somewhat hasty and, hence, unreflected reactions in a time of crisis (for example, inadequate follow-up in connection with dismissals and restructuring). This might be related to events that can be easily remedied, such as, where the necessary manpower is soon made available, through additional staff being brought in. In that case, the situation pertains only to the process aspect in this perspective. If, however, it persists over time, it will lead to structural changes. This might, for example, be the result of constant under-staffing, where the labour resources do not match the workload. Structural conditions in the organisation may, in turn, be related to structural conditions in the larger context, in the form of market conditions, legislative regulation, competition, financial crisis, etc.

In our example, we note that the organisation in question has undergone a rationalisation process, especially since it was taken over by a new owner (an investment fund) a few years ago; in this process, certain departments were merged and downsizing removed a layer of management. This is a key reason for the expanding area of responsibility that "our" manager has been facing.

In the *lower-left quadrant perspective,* we also note the distinction between the process and structural aspects of the stress phenomenon. An example of temporary process aspects would be a situation that led to temporarily increased pressures because the team was a person short; that situation might be handled by everyone pulling together, so that subsequently the situation would be back on track. If the short-staffing persists over time, it might have a more enduring impact on the organisational culture; for example, by creating a negative atmosphere among the employees or a culture of bullying or harassment ("when poverty comes in at the door, love flies out the window"). Any company or organisation has its own culture or corporate spirit. The manager in our example works for an organisation that is characterised by a unique and long-standing spirit of people pulling together, helping each other out, and putting in the extra effort when it is needed.

The staff might try to preserve this culture (lower-left), while structural conditions in the lower-right quadrant might contrast it (for example, here, where the rationalisation process clashes with the old culture and produces conflict).

Intervention and conclusion of the example

Using the quadrant model, in this case we were able to make the manager's superiors acknowledge that the task was too much for one person to handle, and the given area of responsibility was divided up. Thus, as soon as the manager was convinced that the new structure had been implemented, and after a few weeks' sick leave, he was able to return to a new and more realistic area of responsibility with a balanced quadrant profile.

REFLECTION BOX 4

Complementarity and polarity

Polarity and complementarity are key concepts in IGP. Polar (or complementary) phenomena exist by virtue of their opposites, for example, day–night, light–dark, life–death, strong–weak, singular–plural. In our use of the quadrant model, we focus on the polar aspects of the phenomena as expressions of dynamic and complementary entities rather than as separate and contradictory aspects. In doing this, we appreciate and acknowledge the *complementarity in polarities*.

(continued

Figure and ground (see Chapter Three) constitute a complementarity. The figure–ground relationship is the actual unit of analysis, not merely the figure, as it only ever exists in relation to a ground; that is, it is the complementary relationship between figure and ground that constitutes the meaningful unit. Similarly, in practical IGP work, one may focus on the polarity of a given phenomenon and their mutual complementary relationship by enabling a dialogue between the parts (for example, in two-chair work), often with a view to re-establishing the dynamic and complementary unity of the opposites. Complementarity is often to be found in seemingly polar aspects.

In examining polarities in IGP work, such as mind vs. body, strong vs. weak, etc., we may find that they serve to maintain a dichotomy in the person. In that case, they have gone from being *complementary polarities* to being *polarisations*, which implies a lack of understanding of the complementary relationship between the poles; this causes a mutual tendency for them to exclude each other instead of functioning as a dynamic whole.

In the quadrant model, the complementary relationship between psychological and physical phenomena is located in the relationship between upper-left and upper right-side perspectives. Here, to quote Bohr (1961), we may say that

> . . . in associating the psychical and physical aspects of existence, we are concerned with a special relationship of complementarity which it is not possible thoroughly to understand by one-sided application either of physical or of psychological laws. In consideration of the general lessons we have learned from the atomic theory, it would also seem likely that only a renunciation in this respect will enable us to comprehend . . . that harmony which is experienced as free will and analysed in terms of causality. (Bohr, 1961, p. 24)

Bohr's concept of complementarity is generally associated with the discovery of quantum mechanics. However, according to Favrholdt (2009), his interest in complementarity predates this discovery, as it is related to his contact with his cousin, Edgar Rubin, whom Bohr assisted in connection with some of his experiments in perceptual psychology (see Rubin's vase in the chapter on gestalt processes (p. 71). According to Favrholdt (2009, p. 316) "from around 1905 until his death in 1951 [Rubin was] Bohr's closest conversation partner on issues concerning philosophy and psychology" (translated for this edition).

In IGP, we use the quadrant as a means of honing our capacity for recognising co-existing complementary perspectives on a phenomenon, rather than seeking trust purely as seen from any given perspective. *The purpose of honing our understanding of the quadrant perspectives is to develop a greater perspective awareness of co-existing complementary aspects and to "push" the mind to be able to contain multiple polarities at the same time, and to know when one is seeing what and from which perspective.*

CHAPTER TWO

The organism

W hen we use the concept of the organism to characterise the individual, we do it to underscore our understanding of the biological–physical aspect as an integrated part of the individual's interaction with the rest of the field. Due to Perls' inspirations from the neurologist Kurt Goldstein (1878–1965), this integrative view of the relationship between psyche and soma has characterised the gestalt approach since it was founded (Perls, 1969; Perls et al., 1973). In many regards, recent breakthroughs in neuroscience have confirmed that, in terms of neuroanatomy and neurophysiology, the individual's fundamental sense of self is associated with basic body-regulation mechanisms (Damasio, 1999), and that emotions, sensations, and somatic markers have a crucial influence on rational cognitive functioning (Damasio, 1994).

Organismic self-regulation is fundamental

The human organism is self-preserving in relation to the field that it is a part of. In principle, the logic of self-preservation here is the same as that which applies on all organismic levels, even the cellular level of the organism, where the individual cell is designed to pursue self-preservation and growth and is constantly dependent on influences from its surroundings. There is nothing mysterious about that. It is *organismic self-regulation* in the sense that the organism, based on its needs, uses its capacity for thinking, feeling, and setting goals to self-regulate in relation to its surroundings (for example, by seeking out the short-term or long-term satisfaction of needs).

In its fundamental form, a need can be understood as an expression of a state of imbalance or deficiency in the organism. A state of *imbalance* might relate, for example, to the organism's intentionality with regard to its need for growth. Such a state can be observed, for example, in an artist who becomes restless and begins to doubt her sense of meaning when she is not engaged in working with her art. A state of *deficiency* might, for example, occur in the absence of nutrition, expressed as hunger, or it might occur in the absence of love during a person's upbringing. Such states of deficiency would reflect organismic imbalances that the organism will seek to redress, not as a biological machine, but as a lived body with thoughts, feelings, and existential striving (intentionality) that seeks to maintain, develop, and connect with its surroundings.

Proactive and reactive aggression

For Perls (1969), *oral aggression* occupies a central position in organismic self-regulation. He claimed that when infants develop teeth, they enter a developmental stage where they no longer have to accept everything that they are offered with the mother's milk. The teeth enable the infant to chew, bite, taste, and spit out or incorporate and assimilate things that are "not-organism", turning them into a part of the organism.

Perls considered this oral aggression to be a cornerstone in the form of organismic self-regulation, where the individual is an agent who takes responsibility for determining what is or is not beneficial to take in. This logical principle, says Perls, applies to food, to values, and other people's opinions.

The treatment of aggression in organismic self-regulation and growth has been criticised by Staemmler (2009), among others. He argues that we should distinguish between aggression and the explorative–assertive motivation systems. These are two different motivation systems that children might find it difficult to distinguish between, and Staemmler warns that one risks perpetuating the confusion in the field of therapy by claiming that it takes aggression to promote an assertive–explorative motivation.

We agree with Staemmler that one should be critical of the original gestalt theory concepts of aggression. We do not, however, agree that aggression should not be seen as an ingredient in the organism's proactive self-assertion. Rather than rejecting the role of aggression in explorative and self-asserting motivation, we should distinguish between different forms of aggression. Such a distinction is found in some of the feasibly established parts of the psychoanalytic literature, such as Winnicott (1971) and Kohut (1977), which distinguish between proactive and reactive (or destructive) aggression.

Proactive aggression does not reflect an urge to destroy or annihilate oneself or others. It is a natural part of a healthy striving to manifest one's individuality, which is mobilised when the organism, faced with frustrating circumstances and resistance in the field, seeks to preserve its emergent and/or established integrity. Given good-enough childhood conditions, the proactive aggression will develop into a mature and, thus, subordinate component in the organism's self-regulation, which can be mobilised when the organism deems it necessary—for example, when it has to differentiate itself from others, satisfy needs, carry out important tasks, or achieve desirable goals. Precisely because proactive aggression is subordinate to the larger whole of the organism's self-organisation dynamics, it recedes once the organism no longer needs the "drive" that is inherent in aggression.

On the other hand, aggression that is inherently destructive does not occur independently, but is derived from something else. This is a reactive form of aggression that is manifest in connection with impairments or, in some cases, breakdowns of the organism's psychological capacity for self-organisation. Reactive aggression occurs as an element in the organism's effort to preserve itself in circumstances in which it is subjected to traumatic and/or long-term emotional frustration and betrayal by its surroundings. Instead of expressing the primary emotions of hurt that the frustrations have caused, the organism might cover up these emotions with secondary emotions of anger. Reactive aggressive tendencies, which could, consequently, come to dominate the organismic self-organisation pattern, are, thus, not expressions of an innate destructive aggression (as a kind of death instinct), but, rather, *reactive* expressions of unmet and overwhelming frustrations and violations during the organism's upbringing. Strong reactive aggression—unlike normal, healthy, proactive anger—is characterised by being associated with a mobilisation of past violations and humiliations to a degree where the organism's self-cohesion is overwhelmed, and its general aggression management is impaired. In this situation, aggression could grow out of proportion with the current cause of its mobilisation.

The point is that the distinction between proactive and reactive aggression is relevant for understanding Perls' description of aggressive energy as the energy that has to be mobilised in order to "taste" and "take a bite of" the world proactively. Although terms such as "tasting" and "taking a bite of" are metaphorical in nature, it is important to maintain the distinction between different forms of aggression in order to understand both the proactive and the reactive variation of aggression. This is particularly relevant in a therapeutic context, where it is essential to address whether an aggression that is lived out releases and promotes healthy organismic self-assertion in the framework of optimal organismic self-regulation, or whether the aggression reflects a pattern of repetition and avoidance that is incompatible with optimal organismic self-regulation.

EXAMPLE

A person may join one therapy group after another to work with his anger of not being seen as a child. He pounds the pillow and yells at dad again and again and may, in principle, continue to do this for the rest of his life. There are signs that this could have become more of a repetitive ritual, potentially supported by a therapist who mistakenly considers any cathartic emotional discharge therapeutic. In fact, this is "acting out" behaviour that may give the person satisfaction here and now, but which does not lead to any change in his organisational patterns and, thus, fails to help him move forward in his life. In addition, it perpetuates his illusion that expressing anger is, in itself, beneficial.

Organism: concepts

The key concepts in the gestalt approach concerning *organismic self-regulation* and *organismic phenomenology* pertain to the non-dualist view of organism–environment in the IGP approach. They include cognition (thought), conation (striving), and emotion (feeling), which are, thus, bodily rooted and embedded in field contexts: "There is no thought, striving, or feeling without organism", and "there is no organism without field".

The gestalt cycle

Organismic self-regulation takes place in the contact between organism and environment in the form of repeated processes of gestalt formation and resolution. The person's gestalt processes take place via his (partially conscious) mental mediation between organismic needs and factual surroundings, which means that gestalt processes are embedded in, and essential to, our organismic self-regulation. The conceptual basis of this point of view was developed by Perls in *Ego, Hunger and Aggression* (1969). Here, he clarified that organismic self-regulation is not a closed circle of organismic self-centring, but that it unfolds as the management of the relationship between interior and exterior factors affecting the gestalt process. Thus, the process may be initiated by interior as well as exterior stimuli. Organismic self-regulation includes three main movements:

- a stimulus initiated by the organism or the environment;
- progression through the phases of the gestalt process;
- destruction or completion of the gestalt process.

DEFINITION BOX I

The concept of the organism

The organism includes the individual's psychological and biological aspects and their interacting and correlated functions.

Organismic phenomenology refers to the idea that the individual's phenomenology has a biological–organismic basis and, hence, is anchored in the body.

Organismic self-regulation refers to the idea that, based on the given circumstances, the organism will seek its own optimal regulation in the organism–environment field with a view to achieving self-preservation, sociality, and growth.

This is a concept of balance, based on the idea that a gestalt process, in itself, contains a figure–ground formation process as well as a figure–ground resolution process. The overall gestalt process, thus, is a process whereby something from the undifferentiated field is differentiated into figure and ground and then subsequently fades back into the undifferentiated field. There are several variants of models based on this cyclical concept in the gestalt literature. The best known of them is probably the so-called "cycle of energy", also known in variants as "the contact cycle", or "the cycle of awareness". The process components in this cycle are most often referred to as *sensation* (arising from interior or exterior stimuli), *awareness* (in relation to the meaning of the stimulation), *energy mobilisation* (in relation to this meaning), *action* (following the energy mobilisation), *contact* (as the goal of the act), and *withdrawal* (after completion/satisfaction of the contact). Crucially, the process components should relate to each other in the sense that awareness, for example, should be understood as awareness in relation to the preceding sensation and aimed at the subsequent energy mobilisation, which, in turn, should be understood as energy mobilisation in relation to the preceding awareness and aimed at action, etc. This is illustrated by the arrows in Figure 9, and underscored by our use of the word clarity instead of awareness, thereby referring to the clarification of what the sensation is about—which, of course, is done with awareness. A conceptual reason for using the word clarity instead of the word awareness in the model is that awareness has a broader meaning than the clarifying function it has at the particular step in the model following sensation. We will explain that in more detail in Chapter Four in the section on awareness (p. 92).

Exemplified with the physiological need "hunger", the process could follow the following course: the organism *senses* a feeling (body sensation), clarifies what the need is about (in this case, hunger), *mobilises energy* and registers options in the field for sating the hunger, *acts* in the field by preparing a meal, and then achieves *contact* with a need-adequate something outside itself (in this case, food). This something is incorporated and assimilated in the physiological system of the organism, which satisfies the need. Thus, the gestalt process is completed with *withdrawal* and a new state of equilibrium, creating the space in which new sensations can arise.

We find a different version of the cycle concept in Todd Burley's work (Burley, 2012; Burley & Freier, 2004), where the emphasis is on

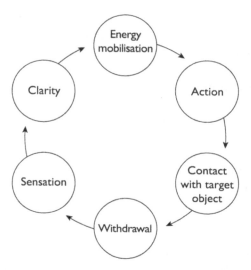

Figure 9.   An illustration of the relationship among the process components of *sensation, clarity, energy mobilisation, action, contact with target, and withdrawal* in the cycle of energy.

the cognitive sub-processes in the gestalt process. The process components in this version of the cycle are *figure formation, figure sharpening, self/environmental scan, resolution* (intending, planning, executing, verifying), *assimilation,* and *undifferentiated field.* Figure 10 illustrates this version of the cycle concept.

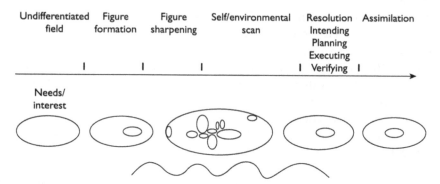

Figure 10.   An illustration of the relationship among the cognitive process components *figure formation, figure sharpening, self/environmental scan, resolution* (intending, planning, executing, verifying), *assimilation,* and *undifferentiated field* in the gestalt process (adapted from Burley, 2012).

Taken from Tønnesvang and colleagues (2010), the process depicted in Figure 10 can be exemplified by imagining a therapist who is focused on working with a client while noting, on the periphery of his attention, an unknown sound in the room. Initially, the sound exists as a fuzzy figure in the gestalt process (*figure formation*). If the sound persists, and his attention to it is increased, the figure is sharpened (*figure sharpening*). The therapist is distracted from his contact with the client and eager to know where the sound comes from and, if possible, to stop it. The therapist looks around the room (*self/environmental scan*) and discovers that it is coming from the new vacuum jug, which has not been completely sealed. The moment he discovers that, the figure changes to *resolution* (intending, planning, executing, verifying) of the situation, as the therapist adjusts the lid on the jug and thus eliminates the sound. *Assimilation* (in the sense of registering the changes in the organism/environmental field that are the result of the resolution of the gestalt formation process) is achieved. For a brief moment, the field is *undifferentiated* (equilibrium), until a *new figure forms and is sharpened* as the therapist again devotes his full attention to the client.

The gestalt process including the phases above will vary in duration. It can range from the almost instant (a few seconds) to the situationally extended (lasting minutes or hours), or to days or years. Each of the component processes may, in some cases, involve incomplete figure formation. The normal progression in the gestalt process may be blocked or interrupted at any point in the sequence. These interruptions might either be in the service of the organism (desirable priorities), or they might result in unhealthy unfinished business in the organism's self-regulation. If a client, for example, inhibits what is, in fact, an appropriate expression of criticism in the therapeutic setting, this could be undesirable and result in unhealthy unfinished business. On the other hand, suspending criticism of a potentially violent person whom one runs into in the street can be a similar form of inhibition that reflects an appropriate priority.

A third version of the cyclical concept describes four stages of contact (Perls et al., 1973, p. 459): *fore-contact–contacting–final contact–post-contact*.

Applying this version to the contact process in interpersonal interactions (see, for example, Hostrup, 2010), the focus is on initial contact exchanges (small talk) and sizing each other up, which naturally precedes the process of exploring possibilities for a potential deeper contact, and the final or full contact which, in turn, is followed by exchanges of a more superficial character, reflecting a closure of contact. This version of the cyclical concept has a natural connection to the ways in which the traditional gestalt literature discusses disturbances in the contact cycle in the form of confluence, introjection, projection, retroflection, and deflection. This understanding operates with five main forms of self-regulation in people's contact with the environment, which can be described as follows.

1. *Confluence* refers to the experience of blurred borders between I-ness and other-ness. Healthy confluence is about a sense of we-ness. In dysfunctional confluence, the individual will have difficulty striking the right balance between separation and connectedness.

2. *Introjection* refers to psychological internalisation and is a precondition of learning. Dysfunctional introjection, in a gestalt sense, compares to Deci and Ryan's (2000) use of the term introjection as a poorly internalised self-regulation style: for example, when someone has "swallowed too much without digesting it", that is, when the person embraces and takes in other people's views uncritically. Undigested elements typically reveal themselves as voices of disintegrated "shoulds" and "oughts", which block organismic self-regulation by interfering with the person's acts. An individual who self-regulates on the basis of dysfunctional introjections will lack the ability to distinguish between his own needs and the needs of others.

3. *Projection* refers to situations where the individual perceives unrecognised parts of his or her self as belonging to the exterior world. Adaptive projection includes taking ownership of the aspects that one projects, trusting one's sense of what is happening in the surroundings. Dysfunctional projection leads to a lack of contact with aspects of oneself.

4. *Retroflection* refers to situations where the energy needed to modify the environment is used against the self and functions to modify the self rather than the environment. Adaptive retroflection is associated with the control of impulses. Dysfunctional retroflection is associated with either inadequate self-restraint or excessive inhibition (and the suppression) of emotions and behaviour.

5.   *Deflection* refers to the capacity for avoiding undesired full contact and remaining calm despite perceived emotional noise. Diplomacy and a healthy sense of humour, for example, rely on adaptive deflection. Dysfunctional deflection prevents the free-flowing exchange of information between I-ness and other-ness that characterises full contact with others.

Although the five forms of contact self-regulation are widely used in the gestalt literature, some of them have also been criticised for being incompatible with field theory. Jacobs (2011), for instance, criticises the concept of projection, with regard to both its implicit understanding that something belonging to the individual could possibly be placed in the environment and the assumption of the therapist's monopoly on defining what constitutes projection. In her view, the concept seems to presuppose a conceptual framework where something is moved from one container to another, which clashes with a field theory concept of the relationship between organism and environment. As she points out we shall—from a field perspective—remain aware that contact regulations are not merely reflections of certain mechanisms in the individual, but include the context in which they appear, including the therapist's share in the mutual contact management.

As mentioned under introjection (point 2), some of the other regulations can be related to theory and research that are fully compatible with field theory, for instance, the self-determination theory of Edward Deci and Richard Ryan (Deci & Ryan, 2000; Ryan & Deci, 2000). Self-determination theory is anchored in a basic organismic–dialectic meta theory which corresponds to our understanding within IGP of the relationship between assimilation and organismic self-regulation. We shall return to this in more detail in the closing section of this chapter. Before that, however, we shall explore the IGP cycle a little further.

The self-regulation wave

With the integrative aspiration in IGP, we use a wave as the basis for incorporating insights from the other versions of the cycle into a coherent understanding. The unique quality of the wave model is that it captures an aspect of polarity that has been less clearly defined in earlier gestalt literature: the polarity between too much inhibition and too little inhibition in organismic self-regulation.

The attention directed towards the two sides of the wave figure was highlighted by the German sociologist Stefan Blankertz (2004) in his social analyses. Blankertz noted the tendency for large groups of the population to show a lack of inhibition in the pursuit of satisfaction of needs. To grasp the gestalt dynamics of people's self-regulation, he stated, we should pay more explicit attention to the balance between inhibition and lack of inhibition, not just in the way we talk about it, but also in the way we theorise about it and seek to measure it, as in the "gestalt type indicator test" (GTI) (Blankertz, 2004).

It is an important quality of the wave model that it illustrates how it is in the relationship between too much and too little inhibition that optimal organismic self-regulation will find its path. This balancing act has a parallel in the relationship between duty and desire, where duty sometimes calls for an inhibition of desire, and desire sometimes calls for a suspension of duty. To achieve a well-balanced life that incorporates both meaning over time (duty) and pleasure (desire) requires balancing to a high degree, where duty and desire do not drive each other out, but find common ground in optimal self-regulation. This is backed up, for example, in modern well-being research, where it is found, with reference to Aristotle's concepts of eudaimonia and hedonia, that it is the transformed relationship between the meaning dimension of existential well-being (eudaimonia) and its pleasure dimension (hedonia) that creates long-term existential well-being (Ryan et al., 2008; Ryff & Singer, 2008).

As illustrated by the wave model (see Figure 11), self-regulation mechanisms that inhibit the organismic energy flow are placed on the bottom line, while lack of inhibition of the energy flow is placed on the top line. In the middle of the model, we find optimal self-regulation, where the energy flows freely as the organism creatively adapts to its surroundings.

EXEMPLIFYING METAPHOR

The middle position in the model might be illustrated by the image of a river, where a canoeist will float most freely and without self-inflicted obstacles in the middle of the river (just as the flow of water in the metaphor we mentioned in the field section finds its optimal and natural course in interaction with the field). If self-regulation is excessively inhibitory, the canoeist will run aground on the lower bank. If the regulation of its energy flow is too uninhibited, the canoeist will instead run aground on the upper bank.

Traditionally, the gestalt approach has focused mostly on the maladaptive *inhibiting* use of contact avoidance (introjection, confluence, projection, retroflection, deflection) in connection with the self-regulation mechanisms. There has been a tendency to tone down the complementary relationship between excessive and inadequate inhibition. This is undoubtedly related to the historical development of the gestalt approach at a time when release from neurotic inhibition was a prominent need for many people. It is, however, (as mentioned) important to note that self-regulation mechanisms also contain a potential dimension of uninhibitedness. This can, for instance, be seen in compulsive gambling, promiscuity, self-harming behaviour, bulimia, and consumerism.

If a person, for example, has inhibited (and, thus, inadequate) contact with his or her own body (the initial sensory phase) or an inhibited (inadequate) awareness of the importance of the need in the subsequent phase, this might impair the person's ability to take care of him/herself, which could manifest itself in polarised fluctuations towards uninhibited behaviour in the subsequent stages of the process. Extreme sensitivity (in the case of inadequate inhibition in the sensory phase), on the other hand, might—in a person's attempts at "self-protection"—manifest itself in excessive inhibition later in the self-regulation process. This awareness enables us to discover the dynamic link between inhibition and lack of inhibition throughout the self-regulation processes.

In Figure 11, we have placed the terminology that characterises the different perspectives on the gestalt process above the illustration of the self-regulation wave. The common denominator for the various models is that they all progress through:

- a stimulus initiated by the organism or the environment;
- progression through the phases of the gestalt process;
- resolution or completion of the gestalt process.

Viewing the wave model in the light of the quadrant model reveals how a person's self-regulation process (through sensation, clarity,

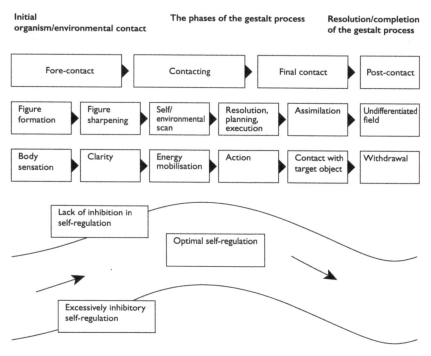

Figure 11. Perspectives on gestalt processes in self-regulation.

energy mobilisation, action, contact with target, and withdrawal) are related to aspects in the four quadrant perspectives. This highlights how organismic self-regulation is constantly influenced by a multiplicity of field factors. In the case of hunger, for example, when sensation becomes figural (corresponding to the point where the figure crystallises from the undifferentiated field) we can examine how the experience of hunger is initiated in an interaction of bodily processes (UR), thoughts, and visions of food (UL), the presence of the sumptuous buffet (LR), and the social aspect of sharing a meal with others (LL).

Because organismic self-regulation progresses with varying emphasis in the respective quadrant perspectives, the self-regulation wave may proceed as illustrated in Figure 12. A body-based (UR) sensation (UL), for example, a gut feeling, signals that one should accept or decline a given assignment. The sensation manifests, or is accompanied by, one's experience of thoughts and feelings in this regard (UL), and, based on these thoughts and feelings, one acts (UR)

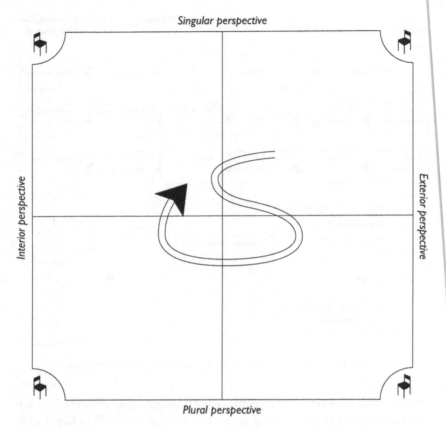

Figure 12. The self-regulation process in a quadrant perspective.

in contact with other objects and individuals (LR). The contact also includes an experiential aspect ("shared meaning") (LL), which forms the basis for one's own experience of closure (resolution and assimilation) (UL).

Optimal organismic self-regulation

As mentioned earlier, organismic self-regulation includes gestalt dynamics and gestalt processes. The gestalt processes that produce the most balanced self-preservation, growth, and development for the organism, thus optimising organismic self-regulation, can be characterised as *optimal* gestalt processes. Over time, optimal organismic self-regulation will consist of continuous progressions of optimal gestalt processes. In correspondence with this point, optimal organismic self-regulation constitutes healthy (from the point of view of the organism) self-regulation in the sense that it is optimal in the present (quadrant balanced) with a flexible reference to the past and an installed consideration for a continued unfolding of life in the future.

Thus, we can define an optimal (or healthy) organismic self-regulation as being a *situationally adequate, future-directed*, and *past-free* self-regulation.

Situational adequacy reflects an optimal sense of realism in the present. In a quadrant perspective, this includes a balanced relationship of left-side phenomenology with conditions and claims in the right-side perspectives.

Being *future-directed* means that the organism has installed an open awareness of the concern for future consequences of present actions.

Being *past-free* means that the organism has a flexible and relaxed, defused relationship with previously established patterns in its gestalt inclination. Thus, being free from the past does not mean being without a past, or being ignorant of the past; instead, it means being so familiar with one's past fixations that one is not automatically (or rigidly) bound to them.

Optimal organismic self-regulation lets the organism attain a natural *awareness–contact–growth* flow. This flow exists optimally when the energy is flowing in the middle of the self-regulation wave (see Figure 11). That is where sensation, need, feeling, thought, and action are naturally interconnected and unfold in an optimal interaction with the factual conditions in the context, in relation both to other people and to the tasks one is faced with. In addition to the question of how to achieve this, organismic balance is also about possessing enough existential competence to be able to deal in a qualified manner with the systems (LR) and cultural (LL) contexts one enters into. More precisely, we should be talking of *existential* organismic self-regulation. Organismic self-regulation, in other words, is not in opposition to, but, in fact, conditioned by, the person acquiring the necessary competences to resolve his or her existence in outgoing and engaged field participation. Hence, the concept of situational adequacy in the definition of optimal organismic self-regulation.

In extension of this point, optimal organismic self-regulation can be understood as a *qualified self-regulation*, which involves an integrated whole consisting of forms of existential competence that are aimed, on the one hand, at technical (technological) system dimensions and social (and moral) cultural dimensions in the field, and, on the other hand, at the organismic resolution of sensitivity (sensation and emotional regulation) and reflection (thoughtfulness and perspective taking).

The understanding that we are presenting here of organismic self-regulation as qualified self-regulation, which is explicit about the need for existential life competence, can be associated with the ideas on qualified self-determination as a concept of Bildung that have been developed by Jan Tønnesvang (2002, 2012b, 2015). The concept of qualified self-determination views existential life competence as a state of tension between outward-directed technicality and sociality, on the one hand, and inward-directed reflectiveness and sensitivity, on the other.

A person will have a technical competence for handling certain tools to be able to do his job. He will have competences enabling him to perform the job in a *systems* setting and, in doing so, also be part of, and have competences in, a social context. As a base for all this, he will have competences for reflection, and for sensing, feeling, and regulating himself. This suggests that organismic self-regulation is a constantly unfolding relationship between an outward field engagement and an inward assimilation and self-appropriation. In the natural flow of *awareness—contact–growth*, one manages the energy in one's use of existential competences, which—further—provides optimal conditions for "being in flow" (see, for example, Csikszentmihályi, 1998).

Mental health is achieved where the energy flows with "ease" as opposed to "dis-ease". However, even if the organismic self-regulation does not serve the organism optimally (for example, in psychopathology, or objectively regarded maladaptive behaviour), the person's behaviour can still be understood and described from an organismic self-regulation perspective. The point is that, on a more profound level, there will be meaning in one's current self-regulation based on the more or less well-functioning existential competences one has developed. Furthermore, it is relevant to take an interest in this meaning or function on a deeper level in order to be able to understand someone's self-regulation and behaviour and help them to change it towards what is also called mature creative adjustment (Yontef, 1993).

REFLECTION BOX 5

Self-regulation: field dynamics and acts of volition

For a person, it seems obvious to view oneself as a being who—at least some-times—acts on one's own volition and choice. Still, most people have also had the experience of acting in situations when they did not really know why they acted as they did, and where they do not really feel that what they did was an act of volition. In the relationship between these two scenarios resides the question of whether people can be said to act on the basis of a free will, or whether they are driven by something else. This is one of the classic questions in both philosophy and psychology, and there have been many proponents and opponents of both points of view. From a field theory approach to organismic self-regulation (which is what we apply in this book), the question of free will is addressed from a complementary perspective that views the individual (the organism) as being both "*in* the field" and "*of* the field".

Attempting an analysis from an "*of* the field" perspective aimed at under-standing all the interacting and subtle causality relations that form the basis for explaining an act such as "going to the opera" (to pick an example) brings us back to the paradox we quoted from Niels Bohr in Reflection Box 4. The paradox is that we have to acknowledge and recognise that there is a complementary rela-tionship between what is perceived as free will and what exists—by virtue of the self-organising dynamics of the field—on the conditions of causality, even if we do not necessarily understand the connection in this relationship.

An exhaustive analysis in an "*of* the field" perspective of the basis for the decision to go to the opera would be infinitely complex and perhaps unfeasible, but if one contends with a simplified version, it would be able to elicit certain key factors, such as, "Listening to/experiencing an opera gives me a good feeling/expe-rience (bodily/neurophysiological); it nourishes my joy in life; it promotes my sense of belonging to a particular socio-cultural group and thus satisfies a need in the socio-cultural field; it gives me occasion to ask my wife out, which secures an adaptive regulation of our relationship", all of which essentially serve the purpose of organismic self-regulation. The core of the matter is that an act such as decid-ing to go to the opera—like the example with the course of the brook (p. 5)—can be understood in an "*of* the field" perspective as the expression of a number of interacting field aspects.

(continued)

In an "*in* the field" perspective, perceived free will is better represented by the concept of *self-volition* (Hansen, 1997), which means accepting ownership and, thus, responsibility for one's actions subject to the degrees of freedom one enjoys and in field relationships whose complexity cannot necessarily be uncovered. In this light, the explanation of the opera example might be to accept responsibility for making a decision to go without implying that this decision is driven by a will that is, philosophically speaking, free in principle.

In practical IGP work, the main key to creating lasting change is to examine how the person's organismic self-regulation takes place. This involves working with the gestalt inclination that exists in the procedural organisation patterns of self-regulation. In the following, we take a closer look at what we call procedural organisation patterns and their formation process.

Procedural gestalt inclination

The role of memory

As Tulving (1985) demonstrated, there are three memory systems where we store our life experiences and the knowledge we acquire. These are the *procedural, semantic,* and *episodic* memory systems. In various ways, the three systems promote our way of functioning in, and managing, our lives. The *procedural* system can be described as a performance system that deals with *how* we do what we do. The *semantic* system is a general knowledge system that deals with what we know about the world and ourselves in general. The *episodic* system is a specific experience system that deals with our memories of personally experienced episodes. According to Tulving, the three memory systems are hierarchically interconnected, with the procedural memory system being more fundamental than, and including, the semantic memory system, which, in turn, is more fundamental than, and includes, the episodic system. Furthermore, each memory system is characterised by a certain form of consciousness or knowledge.

Episodic memory includes experiential self-knowledge (also known as "autonoetic consciousness"), meaning that episodic memory lets us be aware that what we recall is something that we experienced.

Semantic memory does not include experiential self-knowledge, but general knowledge (also referred to as "noetic consciousness") about aspects of the world or oneself. The self-knowledge that might be stored in the semantic memory is not related to experienced episodes, but might, for example, include one's knowledge of belonging to a particular family, or having a particular blood type or eye colour.

Procedural memory includes knowledge that can be characterised as non-knowledge (also referred to as "anoetic consciousness"), meaning that one knows how to do something by virtue of doing it, but that this knowledge is not put into words or related to specific experienced episodes. Procedural memory is evident in specific situations where one functions in a certain way without any conscious reflection on what is remembered on this level. It is a form of knowledge or memory embedded in the body that enables a capacity for doing what we do. A few examples might be riding a bicycle, tying one's shoelaces, or an inclination to have certain thought patterns when one meets certain people without quite being able to explain how and why one does this. The procedural memory is the performance aspect of what is also known as implicit memory—in contrast to explicit memory (Roediger, 1990; Schachter, 1987).

Based on the logic of procedural memory, the procedural gestalt inclination refers to our basis for forming gestalts on a level of consciousness that is embedded in our procedural memory. This implies that we are typically unaware that a certain gestalt process is taking place. It is acquired on such a fundamental level that it unfolds as procedure outside our conscious awareness. According to Burley and Freier (2004), the procedural gestalt inclination is the core of a person's character structure.

EXAMPLE

To exemplify, a young child who is born into the world will naturally cooperate with the key persons in this world, initially the parents especially. The child will adapt to the form that this cooperation takes and will naturally respond to the field as adaptively as possible, even if it means ignoring some of his or her own needs. The child will be prepared to repress and disown parts of himself in order to survive. In a sense, the child responds to, and displays, a capacity and inclination for responsibility (response-ability) to the situation. The child's responses, which are built on his experience-based expectations of his parents' reactions, are stored over time (when the same gestalt process dynamic repeats itself) in the procedural memory. As a result, his future sense of being responsible will match the originally acquired gestalt inclination.

Not all the gestalt inclination procedures that are stored early in life are equally appropriate later in life. For example, this might involve a stored procedure such as "as long as I am nice and pleasant,

REFLECTION BOX 6

The figure–ground relationship in the individual's phenomenology

One of the gestalt researchers who have worked with uncovering the phenomenology of memory in organismic self-regulation is Todd Burley (Burley, 2012; Burley & Freier, 2004). As seen in his model, Figure 13, the organism is part of the field, and it interacts with the field continually (the horizontal arrow). As it is further seen, the organism entails a body-brain, which, in turn, entails the individual's phenomenology. The individual's phenomenology includes the individual's sensation, perception, awareness, experience, thinking, and intentionality.

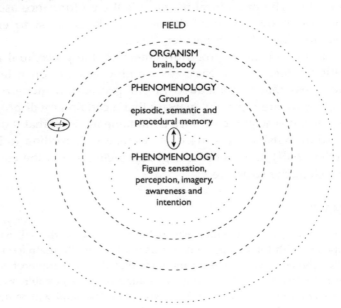

Figure 13.   Interactions among field, organism, and phenomenology.

I will do well in the world", or "big boys don't cry", or "if only I can improve my performance, dad will eventually think that I am good enough". These codes of conduct, or gestalt inclination dynamics, may have a profound impact in shaping one's actions, thoughts, and feelings later in life, although one is unaware of this because they are stored in the (adaptive as well as maladaptive) procedural memory.

The role of internalised self-regulation

As mentioned earlier, the gestalt formation process may be initiated by both internal and external stimuli or influences. The successful gestalt process includes "assimilation", which is the process by which the figure is internalised and integrated (see pp. 46–54). Deci and Ryan's (2000) internalisation concepts let us unfold more precisely how internal and external factors influence the gestalt process and provide an understanding of the assimilation process in the dynamics of organismic self-regulation.

Deci and Ryan (2000) operate with a concept of organismic self-regulation that, as an aspect of fundamental organismic needs, which they call *intrinsic needs*, includes the following psychological needs: *autonomy*, *competence*, and *relatedness*. When we do something that is directly associated with satisfying our intrinsic needs, the act is satisfying in itself. We perform the activity for the sake of the inherent satisfaction that lies in the activity itself. This constitutes *intrinsic motivation*. The other form of motivation is *extrinsic motivation*. This motivation is activated when we perform an activity in order to achieve something other than what is inherently included in what we do. Such motivation, therefore, is governed by something other than the immediate satisfaction of intrinsic needs, and the act is carried out to achieve some subsequent or imagined satisfaction or to meet certain external needs.

The intrinsic aspect, thus, refers to stimuli that are based in the organism's immediate needs and lead to perceived well-being. When I am hungry and eat, the act is satisfying in itself. The extrinsic aspect is associated with the factors that mean that organismic self-regulation can also involve deferred gratification as part of natural organism/ environmental self-regulation. If I do my homework in order to achieve the subsequent gratification of passing an examination, I am driven by extrinsic motivation. If I do my homework because I enjoy it and find myself absorbed by it, I am, instead, driven by intrinsic motivation. Both types of motivation are aspects of organismic self-regulation. It is the way in which we regulate the two types of motivation that forms the key psychological issue in our understanding of organismic self-regulation.

As mentioned in connection with our description of the self-regulation wave, self-regulation mechanisms may work in more or less adaptive or maladaptive ways. An introject that is not subsequently addressed and assimilated exists as a foreign entity, so to speak, that governs the person's behaviour and thinking (for example, as an unnecessary "should"). In Deci and Ryan's terminology, this corresponds to an extrinsic influence that is not fully internalised (for example, in order to earn dad's approval, I am still striving to be a good boy and therefore push myself unnecessarily hard in my job) or properly integrated (in my efforts to be a good boy, I devote a great deal of time to this endeavour, which clashes with my other goals of being a good friend and/or family man and father). When we speak, for example, of "clarity" following "sensation" in the self-regulation wave (where the figure begins to form), it is essential, therefore, to consider how the need that emerges as figure is meaningful in relation to the regulation of intrinsic *vs.* extrinsic motivation.

What determines, in a psychological sense, whether an extrinsic motivation is "good" or "bad" is whether, to what degree, and in what form a particular way of being extrinsically motivated has been internalised, and to what degree it is consequently integrated with satisfaction and the realisation of intrinsic needs.

Hence, the key distinction in our understanding of the relationship between (psychologically speaking) good and bad motivation is not drawn between intrinsic *vs.* extrinsic forms of motivation, but instead between the internal and external regulation of our way of being (extrinsically and intrinsically) motivated. Whether our motivation is regulated internally or externally is, thus, a crucial parameter for understanding how and why individuals are driven (on the level of the procedural gestalt process) to want what they want and to do what they do. It is not simply the case that certain motivations are either internally self-driven or externally driven by punishment/rewards. There is a middle ground where one may be more or less externally motivated despite being driven by internal psychological factors and personal reasons for wanting and doing something.

In their analyses of the spectrum between the external and internal regulation of motivation, Deci and Ryan identify four forms of regulation of extrinsic motivation (*external, somewhat external, somewhat internal,* and *internal*). This is associated with four typical regulatory styles (*external regulation, introjected regulation, identified regulation,* and *integrated regulation*). The logic is as follows.

- *External motivational regulation* means being orientated towards (and adapting to) external standards for rewards and punishment associated with certain acts. This is the type of motivational regulation that the behaviourists focus on. It is associated with an *external regulation* style. An example might be a person who does gardening strictly in order to earn some money or trims the garden hedge merely to avoid being excluded from her allotment garden association.
- *Somewhat external motivational regulation* means being orientated towards introjected images of what one needs to do to avoid feeling guilt or shame over failing to live up to uncritically incorporated standards for proper behaviour that make up the introjected regulation. Although the regulation is enacted by the person him/herself, it is essentially governed by internal foreign bodies that have not been integrated into the personal whole. In Perls' terminology, this is akin to having swallowed something without digesting it, and the result is an *introjected regulation* style. An example would be a person who maintains the garden of the home that he inherited from his parents in order to keep it exactly as his late mother would have wanted it. Even though he never liked his mother's gardening style, he now adopts it, based on an inner voice demanding that this is how it must be done in order to be done properly. The person will feel guilty if he fails to keep the garden in exactly this manner.
- *Somewhat internal motivational regulation* means being orientated towards ego-syntonic values, that is, values that one identifies with and wants to live up to because one finds them appropriate, personally valuable, and in accordance with one's self-images (synonymous with identity or self-narrative). In other words, this is *identified regulation*. The example here would be to create a garden that matches one's own self-perception as a person with a certain style, for example, with garden gnomes and footbridges.

One knows intrinsically what one likes, loves the garden gnomes, and is not embarrassed to talk to others about them. When one trims the hedge at the proper time of the year and keeps it neat and straight, it is because one likes it exactly like that. One identifies with it.

- *Internal motivational regulation* means being orientated, with a high degree of autonomy and self-determination, towards one's holistic self-concept and the personal interests and pleasures one finds in realising oneself as oneself. Internal motivational regulation implies congruence among the various aspects of one's person and is manifest as *integrated regulation*. The example here might be a person who gardens because she finds it interesting and a source of pleasure, because it involves both physical activity and a sense of connectedness with nature, and because she can do it at her own pace and in the manner of her choosing, and, thus, achieve a sense of internal coherence. She likes her garden gnomes, but does not put any particular emphasis on seeing this as an expression of who she is.

In *intrinsic regulation*, one is fully absorbed in the personal interests and pleasure of performing one's current activities. This example almost corresponds to the example of internal extrinsic regulation. The point is that with its markers, integrated extrinsic motivation is largely perceived as intrinsic motivation. The difference is that intrinsic motivation is innate, whereas integrated extrinsic motivation has developed over time.

Deci and colleagues have carried out many empirical studies of motivational regulation styles (Deci et al., 1999). They have demonstrated repeatedly and in a variety of ways that "more fully internalised regulation was associated with greater behavioural persistence, more effective performance, and better mental and physical health" (Deci & Ryan, 2000, p. 241). We do not go into this in any more detail here. Interested readers are referred to www.psych.rochester.edu/SDT/

For the present context, it is interesting to consider how intrinsic needs in relation to *optimal organismic self-regulation* are manifested as values in the person's life management. When life management is viewed in an "of the field" perspective, we may assume that:

- *autonomy* implies that the person achieves self-realisation and owns up to him/herself as he or she is by means of organismic maintenance and growth;
- *competence* implies that the person (has the competence to achieve and) manages self-regulation in a situationally adequate manner, that is, as someone capable of qualified organismic self-regulation (see p. 56);
- *relatedness* implies that the performance of both *autonomy* and *competence* takes place in relation to, and with regard for, others, that is, that the person acts as someone capable of (e.g., has existential competence for) qualified organismic–social regulation. This is further associated with an intentional stance towards the larger whole that one is a part of (corresponding to what Taylor (1991) calls horizons of meaning), that is, with an intentional stance towards larger meaning references (culture, religion, nature, cosmos) that forms the framework for human relatedness (see Tønnesvang, 2012a). According to Hansen (2001a), the dimension of being orientated towards horizons of meaning represents in itself a basic human *need for meaning*, which brings direction to the realisation of the needs for autonomy, competence, and relatedness (see Tønnesvang & Hedegaard, 2014).

These added points about intrinsic human needs, intentionality, values, and existential competence aim to underscore that optimal organismic self-regulation takes place in a larger field context and should, therefore, not be (mis-)understood as a closed individualist process.

Organismic phenomenology and energy

In IGP, we also take a special interest in the energy aspect of organismic phenomenology and self-regulation. With the organismic phenomenological approach, body sensation is given particular attention in the experiences we investigate. Body sensation is fundamental, more or less in accordance with what Gendlin (1981) refers to as felt sense, and which also forms a key aspect in body-orientated forms of psychotherapy (see, for example, Lowen, 1967, 1977) and the somatic experience approach (see, for example, Levine, 2005).

Among the philosophers of phenomenology, the previously mentioned philosopher Merleau-Ponty (1962) is significant in positioning the organism as lived body at the centre of his thinking. The lived body can be viewed as the body's meaning-transcendence of itself as a merely physiological entity (Rasmussen, 1996). The lived body's being-towards-the-world, then, is not merely a collated sum of reflexes, but should be understood as a "pulsating energy" that imperceptibly takes the world into possession in a process where intention is not necessarily realised by a conscious act. Consciousness, to Merleau-Ponty, is not primarily an "I think", but an "I can". In other words, consciousness is predominantly procedural; it is its own performance. The point is that body, thought, and speech make up an organic whole. Thinking does not cause speech—it resides in it. The speaker's speech *is* his thoughts, and speech is a form of expression that is related to embodied expressions such as anger, joy, etc. From that perspective, speech is an organismic expression. We speak–think, finalising our thinking through talk and dialogue.

The internal link between speech and thought that Merleau-Ponty describes is of the same nature as the relational dynamics between psychological and physical aspects that we in IGP assume the existence of with reference to an organismic phenomenology. Like Merleau-Ponty's concept of the lived body as a pulsating energy, we regard the energy concept as an essential element in understanding the relationship between the psychological and physical aspects of the organism. Psychological and physical aspects are what they are, in their various manifestations in and with each other; that is, they are both separated from each other and tied into each other. The link between the psychological and the physical is the so-called subtle energy, which Wilber and colleagues (2008, p. 173) describe as "the missing link" between psychological intentionality (including perception) and physical materiality (including the brain). In certain Eastern body-orientated traditions, subtle energy has been conceptualised as "energy flow" or "chi" and related to energy centres (chakras), energy fields, energy paths, meridian pathways—or, in a combining term, the energy body. A common third in these traditions is that they view subtle energy as essential for our understanding of human life processes and as crucial for organismic health and disease. Although subtle energy cannot be measured with the same physiological certainty as, for instance, mechanical energy, it is regarded as a legitimate study object that is governed by energy regularities with complementary positive and negative energy pathways, in parallel to the workings of electricity.

In healthy organismic self-regulation, the subtle energy flow will be flexible and free flowing, resonating with the psychological and physical aspects of the organism as a whole. If the organismic self-regulation is characterised by psychological blockages, we can think of this as "lumps" and blockages in the energy flow, which could result in psychological as well as physical manifestations of disease. Phenomenologically, it will also be experienced as blockages in the energy flow. The IGP practitioner registers the blockages by paying particular attention to the body aspects of the person's expressions in his or her exploration of the person's expressed phenomenology—for example, with regard to body language. Are organism and expression in mutual harmony? What is the relationship between body, emotion, and action? How is the energy present in this person and in relation to her contact with the environment (for example, in relation to the self-regulation wave, see Figure 11)? How is the character structure expressed energetically and bodily, for example, in posture, breathing, etc.? The underlying premises in practical IGP work for these questions are that:

- self-regulation takes place in the contact between organism and environment as well as within the self;
- self-regulation takes place in an interaction between the organism's sensorimotor functions and contextual factors;
- the self-regulation process, which includes the gestalt process, includes the totality of the perceptual organismic aspects (sensation, emotions, and cognition);
- the self-regulation process involves several phases, as illustrated by the self-regulation model (see Figure 11);
- Energy in this context is understood as interlinking psychological and physical aspects of the organism.

An IGP-compatible angle on the question about the role of energy is also found in Siegel (1999), who, from the point of view of neuroscience and attachment research, argues that the energy concept should be viewed as mediating the relationship between "brain", "mind", and "attachment". In correspondence with both Merleau-Ponty and Wilber, Siegel also challenges the traditional view of *the mind* as a reflection of what happens in *the brain*, rejecting this perspective as untenable. Instead, he argues, the *brain* is shaped by the *mind*, just as *the mind*, in turn, is also shaped by our relational, contextual relationships, by which *the brain* is also influenced and partially shaped.

Taken together the idea is that a process of "energy" influence and exchange takes place between mental aspects, the brain/neural aspects, and relational aspects. We can observe *that* this exchange process takes place, but we cannot (yet) say exactly *how* it takes place, although certain theories do attempt to offer an explanation (see, for example, Hart, 2008; Siegel, 1999).

CHAPTER THREE

The gestalt process

W hen gestalt therapy was developed towards the middle of the 1900s, it emerged as a namesake to gestalt psychology, which at the time had made important discoveries about human perception. As humans, we tend to perceive things in meaningful wholes; thus, we arrive at a meaningful whole (a gestalt), even if what we perceive is incomplete or vague. From a field theoretical point of view, this gestalt concept is generalised in gestalt therapy to mean that people form gestalts of (attribute meaning to and shape) their environment, while the environment (including its history) also, in continuous variation, shapes human beings. In accordance with this, the focus of gestalt work is on the gestalt processes that take place in the field in the contact boundary between the human organism and its environment (and in the mutual contact of aspects in the individual organism). To summarise this understanding, Perls and colleagues (1973) defined the gestalt approach as "the science and technique of figure/background forming in the organism/environment field" (p. 298). More specifically, the investigation is focused on "the operation of the contact-boundary in the organism/environment field" (p. 275).

The core function of IGP work, similarly, is *the study of the gestalt process in contact relations in the organism–environment field*. In accordance with Perls and colleagues, this definition captures the fact that this is a field-orientated approach, and that it is the gestalt process in particular that we are exploring. In Definition Box 2, we specify the meaning of selected gestalt terms.

DEFINITION BOX 2

Gestalt

A *gestalt* refers to a perceived whole that cannot be broken down into smaller elements without loss of meaning (for example, a musical stanza or an action sequence).

Gestalt process (synonymous with "gestalt formation process") is the process by which a gestalt is formed and dissolved. We say that the person *forms a gestalt*, and that a *gestalt process* takes place. Gestalt process and gestalt process dynamics are key elements in the individual's organismic self-regulation.

Gestalt is used as the general term for working with a focus on gestalt processes in a field perspective, for example, in the guise of gestalt therapy, gestalt supervision, and gestalt work.

Gestalt psychology includes the principles of perceptual psychology that the gestalt psychologists (Wertheimer, Koffka, Köhler, Lewin, and Zeigarnik) found applicable to people's and animals' gestalt processes.

Gestalt process diagnostics includes the analysis and description of types of gestalt processes.

As specified in the definition box, a gestalt process is the process by which a gestalt is formed and dissolved. The gestalt process thus involves a figure–ground formation and a subsequent dissolution of this figure–ground formation. This process engages cognitive, emotional, motivational, relational, and somatic processes as well as socio-cultural and system structures, all interacting to produce a meaningful figure–ground formation.

Perceptual and organisational principles as the basis of gestalt processes

The contributions of gestalt psychology: gestalt principles

The key activity in an analysis of the gestalt process is to capture the micro-processes that are at play when something emerges as figure, while something else becomes the background to this figure.

It was the Danish psychologist Edgar Rubin (1915) who articulated the fundamental gestalt principle of perception revolving around figure and ground, as illustrated in Figure 14.

Rubin's vase serves to illustrate the fundamental premise that attributing meaning to something occurs when something emerges as figure in relation to something else, which then becomes ground. There is, thus, a complementary relationship between figure and ground. The figure in the example may be seen as a vase or as two faces. The perception of one or the other depends on the perspective applied by the eyes that see. Thus, the perceiving and the perceived form an inseparable whole. *Gestalt formation is a function of the perceiving and the perceived.*

In addition to the fundamental figure–ground gestalt principle, the gestalt psychologists also identified a number of other principles for the way in which we, as humans, gestalt wholes. Among these discoveries (Wertheimer, 1997[1923]) was the *principle of similarity* (our inclination to perceive figures based on their degree of internal similarity), *the principle of proximity* (our inclination to perceive elements that are close to each other as belonging together), and *Prägnanz*, or *simplicity* (our inclination to perceive figures in the simplest possible way). These three principles refer to the way in which we perceive and form "good gestalts", where the whole (the gestalt) determines the character of the individual elements. Other contributions were Kurt Lewin's and Bluma Zeigarnik's (Zeigarnik, 1997) discovery that incomplete gestalts tend to continue to appear as figures because they call for completion.

Figure 14.   Rubin's vase.

The principle of figure–ground formation and the other gestalt principles were discovered in a context of experimental perceptual psychology. Perls transferred these discoveries to his understanding of how we form gestalts in a broader sense. We make meaning through figure–ground formation and perceive wholes, their shortcomings notwithstanding. It is not unusual for someone to say that they have had a happy childhood, although closer inspection (for example, in therapy) reveals this to be an idealisation. The realities of these persons' life histories typically hold considerable pain, which they have relegated to the background in favour of perceiving a more pleasant figure.

In the context of gestalt therapy, we also sometimes speak of "unfinished business", that is, incomplete gestalt processes that tend to interfere with, and affect, the current gestalt process. A related concept (which is also used within general psychology) is the Zeigarnik effect, due to which it is easier for us to remember and be tormented by interrupted acts and by the things we failed to complete than by things we manage to finish. For example, it is often unfinished situations from childhood that need to be processed in therapy to release energy that has been locked and remove blockages from current gestalt processes. With reference to the phenomenon of stress (see p. 35), for example, the things we *fail* to get done are typically a major contributing factor in creating a stress condition because it is difficult to let go of unfinished and incomplete tasks.

Baumeister and Tierney demonstrate in their book *Willpower* (2011) that the Zeigarnik effect is not about completing gestalts as such. Although what binds the mental energy is indeed unfinished gestalts (as demonstrated by Zeigarnik), the moment one has a plan for future action with regard to grappling with the issue of the open gestalt, the mind finds peace and releases mental energy. This matches the widely known positive effect of to-do lists. Once the many unfinished tasks have been committed to paper on a to-do list, it is easier to take a calm approach to them than if one has to keep juggling them all in one's mind.

With regard to the fundamental principle of figure–ground formation, IGP practitioners are, just like Perls, especially interested in the place where the undifferentiated field is differentiated out into figure and ground. This place is called the creative point of indifference, or creative indifference (*schöpferische Indifferenz*, see Friedländer, 1918). It is called "creative indifference" because it refers to the creative process where the possibilities of what will become figure and how the figure–ground formation will take place, are open.

This is the point where the actual differentiation between figure and ground begins. With reference to the vase/face figure (Figure 14), it may be viewed as the point where the figure formation has not yet begun. Yet, while the figure formation in Rubin's example can only move in two complementary directions, a vase or two faces, respectively, human organismic self-regulation and creative adaptation hold countless gestalt possibilities (that is, figure–ground formations) as a result of complex functions of individual and contextual factors.

The philosopher Salomo Friedländer's (1918) concept of creative indifference (*schöpferische Indifferenz*) is compatible with the gestalt psychologists' discovery of the principle of figure–ground formation, but while the gestalt psychologists focused on the figure formation process, which occurs through differentiation, Friedländer's main interest was with the middle position between the differentiated poles. Instead of simply seeing the undifferentiated (*die Indifferenz*) as a background of little interest, from where the interesting figure might emerge, he pointed out that it is only in the middle that we have the option of directing our attention at a holistic perspective that goes beyond the figure–ground differentiation. The point of indifference is a creative place where the possibility of new meaning-making figure–ground formation occurs, and, therefore, it is also characterised as the creative point of indifference.

Perls (1969) was strongly inspired by Friedländer's ideas, which are manifest in gestalt therapy concepts such as the fertile void, predifference, equilibrium, centring, and polarity. In practical gestalt therapy, there is an effort to integrate dissociated aspects of the person—dissociations that imply a fixation in the person's figure–ground differentiation (a fixed or frozen gestalt). The goal of the practical work is to enable the person to use his or her creative indifference to achieve a higher degree of flexibility in his or her gestalt dynamics as the basis for developing an organismic self-regulation that enables more flexible and situationally adequate behaviour.

It should be pointed out here that the figure–ground concept refers *both* to the differentiation between figure and ground that is involved in a perceptual process *and* to the difference between what the person's awareness is directed at and the background that is not included in the person's awareness.

Previously, we described the holarchical organisation of the field, drawing a parallel between the concepts of a holon and a gestalt. They both refer to a whole that loses its meaning if it is broken down into smaller components. As we have just described, people attribute meaning to *what is* in a way that is characterised by certain particular gestalt inclinations (which can sometimes be explained in behavioural terms as the result of conditioned reflexes). This means that the gestalt we form is not always in complete accordance with the natural holarchical organisation of the field. Gestalt formation may contain aspects of reality that are dissociated, so to speak. That is why there will sometimes be a mismatch between the natural organisation of the field and the perceived gestalts. On this basis, the therapeutic process can be understood as an effort to achieve a better match in this relationship. This also implies quadrant balancing the person's phenomenology with the objective reality (to which the existential conditions belong).

Gibson's contribution: direct perception

Gestalt psychology examined and identified a number of gestalt principles in an experimental context. As Gibson (1986) later demonstrated through experiments that revealed our capacity for so-called direct perception, the organism is not the only frame of reference for the gestalt principles, as the occasion for this organisation also exists in the objective perceived environment. Gibson captured this relationship between the perceiving organism and the perceived aspects of the environment with his concept of *affordances*, which might help us grasp the perceptual basis of seeing gestalt formation as a function of the perceiving and the perceived. He wrote,

> The *affordances* of the environment are what it offers the animal, what it provides or furnishes, either for good or ill. The verb to afford is found in the dictionary, but the noun affordance is not. I have made it up. I mean by it something that refers to both the environment and the animal in a way that no existing term does. It implies the complementarity of the animal and the environment. ... [An] affordance is neither an objective property nor a subjective property; or it is both if you like. An affordance cuts across the dichotomy of subjective–objective. (Gibson, 1986, pp. 127–129)

Thus, affordances are neither absolute environmental characteristics nor absolute subject characteristics. Affordances are relational phenomena and, thus, anchored in both the objective reality and the subjective experiential world. The point is that the organism's perceptual experience and awareness come about precisely because the organism has immediate access to the concrete object with the particular properties that enable the perception of the given affordance.

One practical consequence of Gibson's concept of perception is that we cannot make predictions about human behaviour unless we know the specific situations or contexts that a person exists in, as the perceptual gestalt process is a function of the field as such. The theoretical consequence of Gibson's approach in relation to the ongoing development of gestalt theory is that it offers a foundation for our understanding of the gestalt principles that the gestalt psychologists identified, which is compatible with an "of the field" perspective. Essentially, the organism has a capacity for directly perceiving environmental properties, but it is also equipped with gestalt principles that cause it to create figure–ground formations that are meaningful in relation to its organismic self-regulation. By drawing on Gibson's work, we can supplement traditional gestalt thinking with a criterion for addressing a basic condition for optimal organismic self-regulation: that the relationship between direct perception and the construction of meaning is well balanced, so that the meaning we construct is not detached from our perceptual basis but refers to it for reality testing and reality matching, so that our constructions can serve the creative adaptation between organism and environment in the best possible ways.

REFLECTION BOX 7

Technical details in direct perception

According to Gibson, the reason why the organism's perceptual access to the object is immediate and direct is that perception relies mainly on higher-order variables (also known as "invariances"). Invariances reflect the sort of "geometric constants" that always occur between the stimuli to which the perceiving eye is exposed and the object in the field, given appropriate conditions (in terms of light, sound, viewing angle, etc.). When we move around the field and see, touch, and examine objects, our impressions vary, but because these variations always occur

(continued)

in connection with inescapable invariant factors (for example, that a car is not perceived as smaller as it drives down the road, although the stimuli we receive from the car actually grow smaller, seen in isolation), the relationship between the perceiving organism and its environment will always contain higher-order variables, as Gibson calls it (which is why we see a car moving away from us). These higher-order variables are direct expressions of factual conditions in the field in which the perceiving organism exists. Because it is these higher-order variables, and not elementary sensory data, that form the perceptual baseline, the information about the field that the perceiving organism picks matches the objective conditions of the field directly.

Our perception of the environment is veridical—or valid, to use another term. This is not, essentially, due to construction processes in the mind of the perceiving organism, but due to the fact that higher-order variables provide information about the factual conditions of the environment. In that sense, one can say that higher-order variables are the path by which we perceive affordances. That there is also something going on in the mind of the organism in the sense that pre-formed patterns of organisation influence what we see does not alter the fundamentally direct nature of our perceptual process.

Thus, when Gibson writes that the concept of affordance "cuts across the subjective–objective dichotomy" (1979), it should be noted that the dichotomy is dissolved *in the relationship between subject and object* as a result of the organism's actively explorative *contact with*, and direct perception of, the meaning-making properties of the object. That is, even though perceptual biases can be and are shaped by experience in ways that do not represent the affordances, the brain does come with already predetermined perceptual and meaning biases.

Gestalt in the intersection of organism and environment

In relation to the gestalt process, there continues to be good reason to focus on the relationship between the organisational properties of the organism and objective, measurable data in the environment (the relationship between organismic consciousness and measurable causality). This interest calls for situational awareness. We cannot know what exists in the objective world until we observe it. We are ourselves part of the field (we are "of the field"). The gestalt organisation is not *exclusively* anchored either in the organism or the environment, but is a joint affair of organism and environment that involves both sides as an expression of the organisation of the field.

The gestalt process in IGP

The basic analytical work in IGP is the phenomenological investigation of the person's gestalt processes as they unfold in connection with the formation and resolution of gestalts. Gestalt processes are, as has been described, initiated by organismic needs in a physiological as well as a psychological sense. The person is hungry, and food comes into the foreground. The person feels lonely, and the need for social contact comes into the foreground. What serves the organismic self-regulation tends to stand out as figure, while other aspects become background (see the self-regulation concept discussed above).

When gestalt principles are viewed more broadly in relation to a person's ways of perceiving, conceiving, experiencing, developing, and establishing perceptual patterns, for example, throughout the person's upbringing, this will influence our attempts to understand the person's thoughts, emotions, and actions.

EXAMPLE

When, for example, a neglected child seeks to create a meaningful figure–ground perception of a reality that is characterised by neglect, the child may do so by perceiving that he or she is to blame for the neglectful parents' actions. That might preserve the notion of the parents as loving parents, which, for the child, might be a more tolerable figure–ground formation than experiencing that the persons on whom the child depends fail to provide what the child needs. However, this could also form a figure–ground formational inclination (procedural gestalt inclination) that is stored in relation to the child's future gestalt processes, coloured by a negative self-perception.

Gestalt process diagnosis

An IGP categorisation or diagnostic process will attempt to demonstrate how certain types of gestalt patterns correlate with the traditional diagnostic systems. Traditional and current diagnostic practices in psychiatry, the *ICD-10* and *DSM* systems, revolve around categorisations based on patient behaviour and symptoms—that is, on the outcome of the gestalt process and not on the specific gestalt process that resulted in the symptoms. The traditional diagnosis is based on the way the disease presents, not on the gestalt process that is unique to a particular symptomatology.

With regard to the *DSM* system, there has been growing awareness of the need to revise the diagnostic criteria to bring them in accordance with the aetiology of the distinct diseases. The book *A Research Agenda for DSM-V* (Kupfer et al., 2002), which was part of the research basis for *DSM-V* (released in 2013), points out several weaknesses in the *DSM* system. David Kupfer (who headed the revision process) and his colleagues grouped the weaknesses into three main categories (2002, pp. xviii–xix, 2; see also Wilson, 2008, pp. 150–151).

- First, the goal of being able to validate the common aetiology of syndromes has proved unattainable. Epidemiological and clinical studies have found a high degree of comorbidity among various disorders, which undermines the hypothesis that syndromes represent distinct aetiologies. Further, epidemiological studies have found a high degree of short-term diagnostic instability in the case of many disorders. In relation to treatment, the lack of specificity is more the rule than the exception.
- Second, some researchers' unquestioning adoption of *DSM-IV* definitions has, to some extent, hindered research into the aetiology of mental disorders.
- Third, states and symptoms represent a somewhat arbitrarily defined deviation from normal behaviour and normal cognitive processes, which means that the system pathologises ordinary experiences of the human condition.

According to Kupfer and colleagues (2002), a major part of the problem in viewing the categories of the diagnostic system as equivalent to the diseases is that it tends to obscure, rather than elucidate, relevant research findings. Overall, these points suggest the need for a theoretically based revision of the approach taken to diagnosing phenomena as well as an empirically based one. In spite of the efforts to revise the system, unfortunately, the criticism above can also be raised in relation to the new *DSM-V*.

In relation to this point, it is interesting to consider to what extent the IGP approach with its focus on gestalt process dynamics might contribute—first of all—to enhancing the theoretical basis for this established diagnostic systems. This would require diagnostics to include the course of the gestalt process rather than relying exclusively on its outcome. Special attention would then be directed at understanding the gestalt dynamics that characterise the disease, which means that the diagnostic process would begin at the source rather than the outcome, thus focusing more on the process than on the symptoms it produces.

As pointed out by Burley (Burley, 2012; Burley et al., 2005), it is a central assumption in gestalt process diagnosis that the type and degree of disorder in the organismic self-regulation are associated with the location of dysfunctions in the gestalt formation process. This implies that the basis for distinguishing among different forms of psychopathology is found by uncovering *where* in the gestalt process there is a problem, and *what* aspects of the gestalt process this problem involves (is it related to figure formation, figure sharpening, self/environmental scan, resolution, or/and assimilation). It is on this micro-process level that we find the key for truly distinguishing among specific psychopathologies. Thus, one might find the following psychopathologies.

- Those where figure formation (the sensation of needs) is inhibited or prevented from the outset differ from psychopathologies where the figure is formed but is not maintained long enough to ensure that the need that is reflected by the figure becomes clear enough to enable its satisfaction. An example of the former might be *depression*, which involves limited or inhibited figure formation, corresponding to inadequate contact with fundamental (intrinsic) needs, which, thus, are not met, but instead leave the organism with a sense of helplessness or hopelessness. When the person lacks contact with a need perception that would form a figure, there will be no need-based action and satisfaction (assimilation).
- Those where a clear figure is formed differ from psychopathologies where the figure formation contains a split between two phenomenological worlds that mutually exclude each other. A situation with this form of split is a characteristic feature of *borderline* cases, where there are two separate phenomenal realities, each with its own figure–ground gestalt dynamics. These two mutually exclusive phenomenal realities coexist and produce two parallel gestalt inclinations in the overall gestalt process. When one of these inclinations (and its phenomenological modes) is activated (and dominates), the person's figure formation

process takes on a positive valence, and he or she might come to idealise the IGP practitioner. When the other phenomenal mode dominates, the figure–ground formation has a negative valence, and the person will devalue the IGP practitioner. Due to the split between the two modes, the person will fail to discover how the inconsistency between the two types of processes is reflected in changing attitudes to, and perceptions of, him/herself and others.

- Obsessive–compulsive disorder (OCD) states will be associated with a clear figure formation, but the moment in the gestalt formation process when the self/environmental scan takes place, the clear figure is pushed out and replaced by other figures in the environment. As a result, the original need (the figure that is intrinsically anchored in the organism) remains unsatisfied and cannot be assimilated (see Burley et al., 2005 for additional details).

Procedural organisational inclination and character structure

In IGP, thus, we regard psychological disorders as expressions of dysfunctional gestalt processes. The various disorders are the result of *both* their location in the gestalt process (that is, where in the process the disruption occurs) *and* the typical nature of the disruption. With reference to Burley and Freier (2004), we may say that the implicit inclination to display certain gestalt processes reflects the person's character structure, and that this structure will typically manifest itself in a fairly uniform manner, independent of the context the person enters into. Thus, the character structure will be evident across the person's life situations, and also in therapy settings. Even if different life situations lead to different forms of behaviour, perceptions, and self-perception, the person's way of forming, dissolving, and/or interrupting the gestalt processes will be characteristically stable for this person across situations and contexts. This is why, in IGP, we aim to draw attention to the *typical* tendencies in the person's gestalt processes which make up the person's character structure. In other words, the character structure is the key target of the transformational work in IGP therapy (Burley & Freier, 2004; Yontef & Jacobs, 2008).

REFLECTION BOX 8

Gestalt dynamics in people with schizophrenia

As a parallel to the effort to analyse the gestalt process in connection with mental disorders, it is interesting to note that, back in the 1950s, the German psychiatrist and neurologist Klaus Conrad (1958) carried out empirical studies of soldiers to study gestalt processes and changes in the gestalt process in patients with incipient schizophrenia. Conrad based his work on gestalt psychology, but apparently completely lacked any contact with the gestalt therapy scene. He found that the core point of schizophrenic perception is a change in the person's reference system. The person's perception of abnormal meaningfulness (apophany) and his perception that everything that happens in the world revolves around him (anastrophe) co-occur simultaneously. The background is that the person who suffers from schizophrenia lacks the usual ability to change reference point that most of us generally have: for example, when we discover that it is not the train we are sitting in that is moving but, in fact, the train next to us, as we can only perceive motion in relation to an immobile reference point. People who do not suffer from schizophrenia carry out these shifts in reference point constantly in order to match their gestalt process with the physical and socio-cultural reality.

Another example would be when we think we hear someone calling our name and then discover that they were not calling to us, but to someone else. A person who suffers from schizophrenia has trouble executing this shift in reference system and, hence, develops a sense that everything "revolves around him".

From this perspective, we are dealing with a perceptual disorder, which naturally leads to the manifestations of the person's pathological world: delusions and hallucinations. Viewed in the light of Gibson's theory of direct perception, a person with schizophrenia has a deficiency on the basic level of anchoring perception in reality (the perceptual baseline). Therefore, he is unable to correct his perceptions against reality and, thus, is at the mercy of psychosis.

In agreement with Gibson's ideas, Conrad describes how it is this distorted gestalt process itself that characterises schizophrenia, and, in relation to diagnostics (see the criticism mentioned above), he emphasises that

> as long as the diagnosis is based on behavioural criteria rather than experiential factors, and any kind of "mad" behaviour, regardless of its underlying phenomena, is characterised as "schizophrenic", it will never be possible to achieve uniformity in diagnostics. (Conrad, 1958, p. 161, translated for this edition)

Diagnostics that rely exclusively on symptoms lack a basis for capturing the core (*radix*) in an understanding of the disease. As Conrad points out, our understanding of schizophrenia should revolve around fundamental perceptual disorders rather than around the spectacular symptoms produced by these disorders.

Until now, we have described the fundamental understanding underlying IGP: the field with the perspectives "in the field" and "of the field", the systematised field model with the four quadrant perspectives, the gestalt concepts of the organism and qualified organismic self-regulation, and the meaning of the gestalt principles and procedural inclination. In the following, in extension of this discussion, we will describe how and why *contact*, *awareness*, and *the experiment* constitute key tools in the practical IGP work.

CHAPTER FOUR

Contact, awareness, and the experiment

IGP is object-orientated first and method-orientated next

I n response to being called the founder of gestalt therapy, Perls
wrote in *Gestalt Therapy Verbatim* (1972, pp. 15–16) that he was not
the founder of gestalt therapy, but simply the finder, or re-finder,
of it. Gestalt processes are a function of the world. Thus, the gestalt
therapy articulated by Perls is not, in its essence, method-orientated,
but, rather, object-orientated, dealing with processes that actually take
place.

Even though gestalt processes are expressed in different ways in
different time and cultural contexts, the principles of the gestalt
process are constant, and it is the process dynamics of these principles
that are in focus in gestalt work. In other words, it is these process
dynamics that are the object of the approach.

The best way to understand a process is to examine *how* it
unfolds as it unfolds. Treating the process itself as the central focal
point leads to a special interest in the *process aspects of any structure*.
In other words, as IGP practitioners, we are curious about understanding which processes are embedded in the given structures we
address. This means that we are curious about the two sides of the

individual's phenomenology. On the one hand, this includes the struc-tural aspect of the phenomenology in the form of the procedural gestalt inclination that is evident in what is commonly known as old patterns, habits, or "baggage", which refers to one's *typical* way of thinking, feeling, and acting. On the other hand, it involves the phenomenology of the process in the form of the *current thoughts/ emotions/perceptions* that exist right now, and which vary constantly. Current thoughts/emotions/perceptions always emerge as figure out of the mental ground, the substance of which is memory, especially procedural memory. That is the fundamental principle of the ges-talt process and, correspondingly, the concept of *procedural gestalt incli-nation* refers to the relationship between the *process* of the current gestalt formation and the *structure* of the mental ground. In the concrete work with gestalt processes, the main focus will be on *how* they take place in the *contact* boundary of the organism/environmen-tal *field*.

The IGP practitioner continually shifts his or her awareness between the processes that play out here and now and the way in which they engage with the person's gradually emerging mental structures. The IGP practitioner's knowledge and experiences with similar types of structures form the background of his focused atten-tion. The practitioner, thus, is neither lost in the here and now nor in pre-conceived professional knowledge, but uses her knowledge of process to enhance her focused attention to the here and now. The goal is to re-establish optimal organismic self-regulation in the person or persons one works with. The means to achieve this are *contact*, *awareness*, and *experimentation*, which will be explained in this order in the following sections.

Contact border and contact boundary

As it is important when working with human contact to be able to distinguish between, on the one hand, the more impermeable borders (such as the extent of one's physical body) and, on the other hand, the more flexible movements that constantly take place in the con-tact between oneself and others, in IGP, we draw a distinction between *border* and *boundary*. While the term *border*, in a psychol-ogical sense, corresponds more or less to the structural aspects of the mental organisation, *boundary* (where people continually and mutually find an appropriate contact) corresponds to the process aspects of mental functioning. The point is that one should be aware of one's borders in order to be able to achieve a well-functioning boundary.

In the following, we will deal with the contact boundary in relation to the process aspects of contact. We also point out that it is always relevant to examine the relationship between the process aspect and the structural aspect.

Contact as the core of the gestalt process

In IGP, the word "contact" is used in a broad sense about all the aspects and processes that take place in the intersection (contact) between organism and environment. It is also in this intersection that the gestalt process takes place, which matches the interrelated nature of contact and gestalt process. The phases in the gestalt process were discussed earlier in the book using a variety of models (Figures 9, 10, and 11) and descriptions in the section on organismic self-regulation, where we also discussed the fact that the contact occurs in the *contact boundary* between organism and environment—for example, the contact boundary between client and therapist. However, we can also talk about contacting aspects inside ourselves, as in "I was able to contact my vulnerability", or "He has difficulty getting into full contact with his body".

Contact is, thus, both about the organism relating to something in its environment and about the organism relating to aspects of itself. In IGP, we capture this duality of the contact concept with the following definition: *Contact is an exchange of information between I-ness and other-ness* (Tønnesvang et al., 2010, p. 588). Given that we always exist in a complex field that we both influence and are influenced by, contact processes are the key to understanding how these mutual influences take place. Matching the definition of contact as the exchange of information between I-ness and other-ness, contact processes are not merely an expression of something that unfolds between one person and another person or between a person and something else within the field (for example, a table). Contact is also about exchanging the information inside the organism that makes it possible, in a first-person perspective, to have a sensation in one's foot or to create an experiential relationship with an emotion.

From a definition point of view, the IGP contact concept does not distinguish between the physical, social, or psychological spheres. That makes it possible to work with contact in the practical IGP relationship (the social sphere) without dichotomising the exchange of information within this relationship in relation to the exchange of information in the person's psychological (and physiological) sphere. We can, therefore, apply the term across the four quadrant perspectives. A quadrant analysis of the contact concept further lets us identify four different meaning aspects related to the four quadrant locations. We return to this point below. For now, we should point out that the definition of contact as an exchange of information between I-ness and other-ness does not, in itself, say anything about the relative importance of various information exchanges (Tønnesvang et al., 2010). If a client makes a comment about the weather, and the therapist nods affirmatively, this constitutes contact in the sense of an exchange of information. It may be considered a superficial contact without any further therapeutic implications, or it may be considered a first step in a trust-building process between client and therapist. As is the case in all aspects of contact, an IGP therapist should pay special attention to the client's contact patterns. If the more superficial contact level reflects the client's inclination to avoid contact with conflicted themes, and if the therapist draws attention to this avoidance strategy, the client might actually experience a deeper contact with the therapist (a feeling of being seen). This greater depth may support the client's contact with the origins of an avoidance pattern (a procedural gestalt inclination) and with the character of the gestalt process of this pattern.

It is a key tenet in IGP that it is the exchange of information with other-ness that enables development and meaning-making for the individual organism. It is, therefore, a natural consequence of the theory that the IGP-practitioner works with dialogue, contact, and contact regulations in therapeutic, supervision, and consultative processes. In other words, IGP theory and practice rely on the same premises in their theoretical or practical efforts to investigate gestalt processes, as they unfold in contact connections in the organism–environmental field

Quadrant analysis of the concept of contact

Carrying out a quadrant analysis of contact will shed light on certain ways in which the exchange of information between I-ness and other-ness takes place (that is, between the aspects one perceives as belonging/not belonging to oneself). Placing contact in the middle of the quadrant model allows us to illustrate how it can be regarded in relation to subjectivity, behaviour, intersubjectivity, and system relations. It also sheds light on what is required to achieve optimal contact in each of the four quadrant perspectives. This is illustrated in Figure 15 and described below.

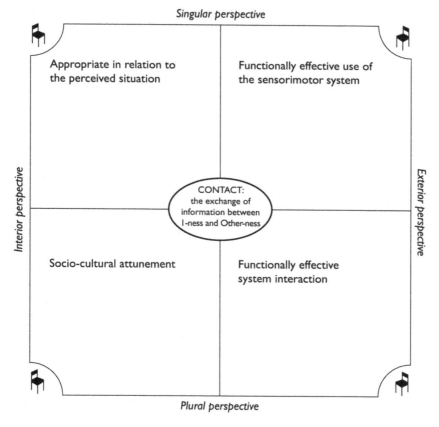

Figure 15.   Quadrant analysis of the contact concept.

Exterior singular perspective (UR)

In this quadrant perspective, the therapist notices how the individual uses his or her senses and motor functions as contact functions in organismic self-regulation. Our abilities to sense (taste, smell, see, hear, touch) serve as contact functions between I-ness and other-ness. Similarly, motor functions are an important part of the contact functionality, as it is through movement we touch and are able to confirm our connection with various aspects of the field. This corresponds to the point in Gibson's theory about direct perception, where organismic perception is typically enlisted in movement and contact with what we perceive. As the term suggests, contact functions are *functional* in relation to establishing and maintaining contact.

In working with people who limit their sensory capacity and, thus, their contact capacity, the practitioner might, with reference to the upper-right quadrant, use the metaphor that "the person has no eyes" if he fails to face facts, or that "he has no ears" when there are things he does not want to hear. The interruption of a body movement may also be noticed in the exterior singular quadrant perspective. Situations where the person fails to complete a movement may sometimes relate to a disruption of the lived body's living out an emotion: "What would your hand do if you were to continue that movement, and what emotion would it imply or release?"

Socialisation affects the way in which we use our senses and our motor system and shapes it towards our sensing and acting with certain purposes in mind: for example, "I see the computer because I need to check my e-mail." Our immediate sensory capacity becomes associated with functional purposes, which could restrict or narrow our use of the senses and dull the senses that play a less functional role. Western culture attributes more importance to the visual and auditory senses than to our sense of touch, taste, and smell. Similarly, it can be argued that "being" (the immediate sensory perceptual sphere) tends to be pushed more into the background in favour of "doing", which might tone down the importance of being in contact with sensory impressions.

In the upper-right quadrant perspective, we also notice the adaptive body-structural aspects of organismic, contact-inhibiting behaviour. If a person has experienced continual anxiety-provoking contact during his upbringing, he might have learnt to keep his head down and stare at the table when he meets other people, a stance that few will perceive as an invitation to contactfulness.

It is also in the upper-right quadrant perspective that we may notice restrictions in breathing, which often have their origins in conditions where the person—in order to avoid feeling powerful emotions and emotional expressions—has learnt to express his or her body sensations and energy mobilisation by inhibiting his or her breathing. Thus, restricted breathing in connection with physiological excitement has become part of a restriction of the person's emotional life.

Interior singular perspective (UL)

The central point here is that thoughts and emotions should be meaningful in relation to the context and appropriate in relation to the person's sensory perceptions. This requires the full use of one's senses, as discussed above, but also the feeling of "having permission" to use them or—in relation to the example above—to dare to risk renewed contact engagement. Contact in this interior singular perspective is, thus, about not avoiding contact with the many different emotions that life occasions, including the unpleasant. The person's procedural gestalt inclination might, for example, keep the person from daring or allowing him/herself to see, hear, smell, feel, etc., which, of course, makes it difficult to feel and think in accordance with what it would be relevant to sense. By suppressing one's contact functions, one may restrict one's "I-boundaries" (that is, what one is able to identify as I-ness in contrast to other-ness).

Exterior plural perspective (LR)

Here, the focus is on achieving functional and effective systems' interaction among the involved parties, that is, having a *shared contact boundary* that lets them send and receive on the same frequency, meaning that they can communicate and, in a purely technical sense, "understand" each other, and that this communication is as efficient and effective as possible. The point is that contact requires a degree of reciprocity, and, thus, that the other's readiness to be seen and heard has a major impact on the person's ability to see and hear.

Touch as a physical manifestation can be the strongest and most rewarding, authentic form of interpersonal contact, but it can also be

the most irrelevant or the most intimidating, involving a risk of domi-
nance or sexuality. Physical touch can also act as a substitute for
contact rather than the opposite. Sometimes, one is *touched* by the
person's voice or gaze, which is then an indicator of contactfulness.
What we see in the lower right perspective is the physical touch itself
between two people. The potential meaning of the touch is to be
understood in either the upper-left quadrant as the individuals experienced meaning, or in the lower-left quadrant as a shared meaning.

Interior plural perspective (LL)

Here, the focus is on assessing whether the perceived meaning is
appropriate in relation to the context and the common frames of reference for understanding meaning. If that is the case, the technical
capacity for mutual understanding may manifest itself in shared
perceived meaningfulness, where the involved parties have mutual
experiences of being in contact. This generates *psychological oxygen*
(Tønnesvang, 2012b) in the relationship between the participants, who
nourish their "need for *relatedness*" (Deci & Ryan, 2000) and, thus,
facilitate perceived existential affirmation and development. In the
IGP therapy relationship, the IGP practitioner relies on personal presence and sincere interest to seek to create an atmosphere (somewhat
akin to a situation with secure attachment) that promotes the person's
capacity for expanding his or her habitual I-boundaries and fixed
procedural gestalt patterns. In the field of psychotherapy, it is generally this perspective on contact, the shared phenomenologies, which
is referred to in talking about the contact between client and therapist
or about "the therapeutic meeting".

DEFINITION BOX 3

Contact

Definition of contact. Contact can be defined as an exchange of information
between I-ness and other-ness.

Contact borders. In IGP, we distinguish between contact *borders* and contact *boundaries*. Contact *borders* are the fixed *borders* (structures that help define contact
possibilities), while contact *boundaries* refer to the processual (and dynamic)
boundary that emerges continually in the interaction in the contact interface.

(continued)

Contact represents both the separation and the connectedness of organism and environment.

Contact regulation (also sometimes referred to as contact interruption, self-regulation mechanisms, or defence mechanisms) takes place in the contact interface between organism and environment. The classic gestalt therapy literature describes the basic forms of contact regulation as confluence, introjection, projection, retroflection, and deflection.

The process aspect of the contact concept can be described in the following phases: fore-contact–contacting–final contact–post-contact.

Contact is both end and means in IGP.

The IGP practitioner's own contact between I-ness and other-ness

The person's gestalt process takes place at the contextual organism–environmental contact boundary and can only be understood in relation to the given context. In therapy, a crucial part of the here-and-now context is the situation that involves the therapist and client, and the focus is on the contact that exists between them, as seen from all the quadrant perspectives. As a therapist, the IGP practitioner will be aware that his own lived gestalt process makes him an environmental factor and, hence, by interacting with the other person (the client), invites her to discover patterns in her own lived gestalt process. In order to keep the person's gestalt process in focus in these interactions, the practitioner's own gestalt process should be as transparent as possible (and ideally free of any maladaptive procedural gestalt inclination)—transparent first of all to the practitioner himself, but also, ideally, to the other.

It is with the purpose of achieving this transparency that the IGP practitioner, via personal development work, should achieve thorough knowledge of his or her own gestalt dynamics and gestalt inclination. The practitioner's own therapy optimises this self-insight, awareness of I-ness and other-ness, capacity for awareness and contactfulness as well as gestalt flexibility and the ability to explore "the creative indifference" together with the persons he or she works with.

The reason why contact is assigned such a central role in IGP is that change is driven more by contact relations than by the person's desire for change. It is, as we have discussed before, an inherent aspect of field theory that the uncovering of field relations, when they are acknowledged (that is, when one gains contact with them), in itself provides access to change. Beisser (1971) pointed this out with his famous phrase: *Change occurs when you become what you are, not when you try to become what you are not.* Polster and Polster specify this point in relation to the contact concept in the following observation:

> In contacting you, I wager my independent existence, but only through the contact function can the realization of our identities fully develop ... Through contact, though, one does not have to try to change; change simply occurs. (Polster & Polster, 1973, pp. 99–101)

It is, thus, essential to emphasise that contact between I-ness and other-ness not only separates, but also forms the basis for connecting what is separate. Contact by means of *exchange of information* is the main source of change. The occurrence of change may be hindered or promoted by a variety of means, all related to regulating the degree of contactfulness. To avoid interrupting oneself during this experience, one must unlearn the restrictions on contact with what *is*, or acquire possibilities of being in contact with it, and avoid limiting one's capacity for contactfulness between I-ness and other-ness unnecessarily. This is important in relation to all four quadrant perspectives.

Awareness as a means and an end in IGP work

The contact concept is closely associated with the concept of awareness, which, as mentioned earlier, is another of the three key components in IGP work. Awareness is always awareness of something, and, hence, also implies *contact* with this something.

Awareness refers to the sense of knowing or registering what is happening while it is happening. It is a kind of "knowing one's doing while doing it". More precisely we can say that, awareness can be defined as *experiencing the registration of difference and movement between I-ness and other-ness* (that is, in the contact boundary). Described in this way, the meaning of awareness is close to the meaning of what Damasio (1999) calls "core consciousness". According to Damasio, core consciousness is the organism's sense that something is happening via its relationship with something other than itself. In the same way, being aware (as a process) is related to the object of the specific awareness (sensation, emotions, thoughts, etc.).

In relation to the IGP effort to change gestalt processes, awareness is the means by which the individual comes to know (the problems in) the phases of the processes of figure–ground formation and resolution. This parallels what Teasdale and colleagues (2002) refer to as metacognitive insight. At the same time, awareness is also an end in itself, as it is often by becoming aware of what is happening, as it is happening, that organismic self-regulation unfolds most smoothly.

In accordance with the point that gestalt therapy is a how-therapy, the IGP practitioner's awareness focus is often on the process itself ("how" what happens, happens).

DEFINITION BOX 4

Awareness

Awareness can be defined as the experience of registering difference and movement between I-ness and other-ness.

Being aware (as a process) relates to the object of the specific awareness (sensory impressions, emotions, thoughts, acts, etc.).

Awareness exists in reflective and pre-reflective forms. This means that one can be more or less aware.

Awareness is constituted by proto-awareness. Proto-awareness is the non-experienced, organismic registering of difference and movement between I-ness and other-ness. Awareness is the experience of this registering (see p .95).

Awareness can be focused or defocused (panoramic), and one can direct one's conscious attention to shift one's awareness from one aspect to another.
One may achieve increased mindfulness by means of awareness training.

Awareness is both a means and an end in IGP.

The goal of practical IGP work is to help the people with whom one works to capture and experience the gestalt process as it takes place here and now, through awareness, in the contact with the practitioner. The point is that the contact between practitioner and the person nourishes the person's capacity for being in contact with, sensing, knowing, and accepting the figure–ground formations that take place from moment to moment (Yontef & Jacobs, 2008, p. 35); to the extent that the person enhances his or her awareness of these changing figures, the organismic self-regulation is optimised. This, in itself, will loosen the rigidity in the person's gestalt inclination.

Awareness work is the primary means for uncovering the gestalt process and discovering how (and why) a person forms gestalts the way he or she does. It is via awareness that the IGP practitioner and the person gain access to the person's sensory and immediate perceptual level, where the gestalt process originates. Initially, the person will be more or less in contact with the immediate sensory aspect (body sensation, emotions). He or she will also typically present the practitioner with diversions from the sensory aspect in the form of thoughts and interpretations (interpretation understood as the meaning—that is, the outcome of a cognitive process—that the person attributes to his or her sensory impressions). Generally, the better the person's contact with the sensory experience, the more the cognitive process, adequately associated with the sensory experience, will be activated. That is one of the reasons why it is important to "come to your senses and use your mind", not only—as Perls famously put it— to "lose your mind and come to your senses".

In the gestalt therapy literature (e.g., Stevens, 1971, p. 5–6), the relation between awareness of sensory aspects, cognitive aspects, and field aspects is conceived as awareness in the inner zone, the middle zone, and the outer zone. The *inner zone* is awareness of one's own body sensation and needs (those aspects of upper-left quadrant which have a clear reference to upper right, e.g., what you sense and feel in your body), the *middle zone* includes all forms of mental activity (which refers to the cognitive/reflective aspect of upper-left quadrant), and the *outer zone* is awareness of one's surroundings (this is the person's awareness of the two lower quadrant aspects). As part of developing a smooth self-regulation, one must have the capacity to switch flexibly between the three zones of awareness.

Situations where the organism regulates itself without acknowledging cognitive processes in relation to what is going on may still imply awareness, albeit in a more subtle form. The relationship between subtle and acknowledged awareness is constantly in play as a relationship among awareness forms mutually influencing each other. This can be exemplified through an excerpt from a therapy session in which an unfocused pre-reflective awareness gradually changes into a more focused reflective awareness.

> *The person* (to the IGP practitioner): "When I left here the last time, I felt good. I didn't think about it until later. But I can tell that something has changed, even though I can't really tell what it is. I think it has to do with the fact that I was late last time, because my bicycle had a flat tyre. I felt bad about being late. But I decided that I wouldn't say anything about it. I think I was embarrassed. You said something I don't quite remember— but it was more about your attitude or the way you said it. To my ears, it sounded like a sort of acceptance."

Without the person's reflective awareness about the content, the interaction between the IGP practitioner and the person contained a form of subtle pre-reflective awareness in the contact process, which provoked and affected the person's gestalt process.

The double duality of the concept of awareness and its anchoring in proto-awareness

The concept of awareness contains a double duality: of *focused and defocused awareness* and of *reflective* and *pre-reflective awareness*. In the terminology of this book, we also use the term *bodywareness* as a synonym for *pre-reflective awareness*. We do this in order to emphasise the embodied nature of pre-reflective awareness.

We also introduce *proto-awareness* as being the constitutional basis of both pre-reflective and reflective awareness. Proto-awareness refers to the occurring, but unperceived, registration of difference and movement that occurs in awareness. Awareness (reflective and pre-reflective) involves the experiential quality of the registration of difference and movement that occurs in proto-awareness. In this sense, awareness is essentially the experience of proto-awareness. The relationship between proto-awareness and awareness corresponds more or less to the relationship between proto-self and core self that is described by Damasio (1999). Proto-self is the condition for the presence of a core self, and, unlike the core self, the proto-self does not include consciousness. On a proto-self level, one does not *experience* one's being.

This experience only occurs on the level of the core self. Similarly, one does not experience the registration that occurs on the level of proto-awareness. The moment that the experience of the registration occurs (the level of), awareness has been achieved.

Let us look at another example which illustrates how the practitioner uses focused awareness as a therapeutic tool, and how awareness can be used to shift attention away from the person's own *interpretation of the sensation* back to *the sensation itself.*

EXAMPLE

Person: "I can tell that I am concerned about my mother's cancer condition."

IGP practitioner: "What are you aware of right now, as you are telling me about your mother's condition?"

Person: (begins to cry, as the questions draws his awareness to the emotion) "I am sad and scared."

IGP practitioner: "Where in your body can you feel that you are scared?" (Shifts awareness to the body aspect).

Person: "Here." (Points to his stomach—the crying intensifies.) "I am scared that she is going to die in pain just like my father did."

IGP practitioner: "Tell me about it." (New aspects of the person's phenomenology unfold.)

Person: "I feel this knot in my stomach just like I did then, and that means that I'm afraid to relate on an emotional level to my mother right now, even though she really needs it . . . I never told anyone how awful it was, the way he suffered." (Awareness of the body aspect activates new memories that have been turned into background in the person's gestalt process; by virtue of this new awareness, they now become foreground).

IGP practitioner: "Tell me about it." (The practitioner offers the contact-fulness that helps the person bring awareness to fixed gestalt patterns, which makes it possible to loosen them.)

By bringing the person's awareness into contact with additional involved field aspects of his experience, the person is able to gain insight into additional aspects of his gestalt process.

Contact and awareness

Contact and awareness are interconnected in the sense that when we become aware of something, we also get into *contact* with it. Similarly, if we get into contact with something, it typically means that our awareness is activated in relation to this "something". As illustrated by the example above, however, contact may also occur without any real or reflective awareness.

As mentioned in the section above, contact involves both a distinction (separation) between the parts that are in contact and, due to the *exchanges of information*, the possibility for assimilation between the two parts (in the form of *fusion* or a process of *internalisation*). From the individual's perspective, the separation aspect can be perceived as what we previously referred to as I-ness *vs.* other-ness. In IGP work, then, the goal is (by bringing awareness and contact to thoughts, emotions, and body sensations) to investigate to what degree it is perceived as meaningful to attribute these thoughts, emotions, and sensations to I-ness or other-ness. This is done, in part, by exploring the processes that have brought about this separation between I-ness and other-ness (the process) and, thus, revising what is meaningful for the organism to assimilate and what is not.

REFLECTION BOX 9

Concentration therapy and inner silence

Perls originally called the method of gestalt therapy "concentration therapy", in contrast to the "association therapy" of psychoanalysis. By concentration therapy, he meant a method for probing more deeply into the essence of the gestalt dynamics. Here, the Latin *con-centratio* can be translated to *with centring*.

One of the means of addressing access to the essence of the gestalt dynamics will be awareness training and meditative and mindfulness practice. Thus, Perls writes in his first book, *Ego, Hunger and Aggression* (Perls, 1969):

> There is one way we can contact our deeper layers of existence, rejuvenate our thinking and gain 'intuition' (harmony of thinking and being): Internal Silence . . . Perhaps the most valuable outcome of the training in internal silence is the achievement of a state beyond evaluation (beyond good and bad), e.g. a genuine appreciation of reactions and facts. (pp. 255, 258)

(continued)

Here, Perls refers to the meaning of going beyond and suspending the man-made duality, polarisation of the fragmentation of reality that accompanies our gestalt process of figure–ground formation. The point is that the figure–ground formation itself might restrict the genuine experience of what *is* and, hence, also restrict our ability to observe how the gestalt process takes place.

Con-centration in the sense of *with centring* thus also relates to the creative point of indifference (*schöpferische Indifferenz*) as described in the section on the gestalt process (p. 69) and to the middle position in the self-regulation wave as described in the section on the organism (p. 41).

Awareness training and awareness competence

In meditative training practices, we can use awareness and contact with emotions, thoughts, etc. to enhance our capacity for separating ourselves from them, that is, to objectify them as belonging to other-ness. The thoughts and emotions are *not* me, but, even so, it is only by being aware of them and in contact with them that I can separate myself from them (through dis-identification or defusion) to avoid being attached to them. In recent years, Kabat-Zinn (1993, 2005) has introduced the Buddhist concept of mindfulness as an important tool and goal in the third wave of cognitive therapy. In this context, the concept of mindfulness is used as equivalent to Perls' use of the concept of awareness. Thus, currently, the concept of mindfulness seems to mark a revitalisation of Perls' focus on the importance of addressing awareness as a key tool in psychotherapy and in human life in general.

Awareness training (in the form of, for example, body awareness and mindfulness training) also, in itself, promotes a healthy figure–ground formation process. The point is that this sort of training promotes the fundamental organism-founded phenomenological intentionality and, thus, the healthy organismic self-regulation that equals a figure–ground gestalt process that serves the organism opti-mally (cf. the section on organismic self-regulation, pp. 41–42).

Enhancing one's awareness competence reduces the risk of fixed or frozen gestalt dynamics, which allows for a more flexible (and, thus, healthier) gestalt inclination. Mindfulness research has found evidence that this type of training is effective in the treatment of depression and anxiety (Hofmann et al., 2010; Piet & Hougaard, 2011).

In IGP, our view is that awareness training promotes access to loosen the "lumps" in the gestalt process, which enables a purer and more flexible gestalt process. With reference to the self-regulation wave (Figure 11) this means that the energy can flow more freely in the balanced middle of the wave pattern. This allows for a more qualified balance between desensitisation and sensitisation. The purpose is to make the gestalt process reflect more closely the requirements of the current situation in contrast to a gestalt dynamics that is governed by old, maladaptive patterns (a maladaptive gestalt inclination).

In Appendix I, we offer a more detailed description of what IGP awareness training involves. As is the case in the work with awareness in IGP intervention practice, IGP awareness training also involves both *non-focused* and *focused awareness*.

1. *IGP awareness training.* Awareness training (like mindfulness training) has a healing effect in itself. Awareness training will also have a preventive function. As the bodily and the mental/ psychological phenomena offer two perspectives on the organ- ism (respectively, the upper-right and the upper-left quadrant perspective), the training may be focused on both enhanced body awareness and techniques that aim to address the mental aspect: that is, various meditation techniques. It might also involve train- ing that addresses energy aspects and movement awareness, such as martial arts.

    Thus, awareness training—for example, in the form of medita- tion—is relevant for the person as an ongoing mental hygiene practice that promotes healing as well as prevention. Further- more, such a training practice will often bring awareness to psy- chological issues that might require professional therapeutic intervention. For the IGP practitioner himself, meditation and awareness training will be essential for maintaining and devel- oping one's awareness capacity as a foundation for one's thera- peutic competence.

2. *IGP intervention practice.* Awareness is the key practice tool in both therapeutic practice and interventions on other levels and in other contexts besides therapy. Awareness is key to everything that happens in IGP. In all the macro- and micro-processes that take place in IGP work (intrapsychically, interpersonally, and in the field as a whole), it is enhanced awareness that produces a

better understanding of the gestalt process and, thus, facilitates change. The IGP practitioner, therefore, uses awareness actively in the intervention process, as both a searching tool and a tool for connecting field aspects (see the example above).

The experiment as an intervention method

In IGP, we are especially focused on the figure–ground formation process that unfolds in the relationship between the phenomenological ground (the organism's procedural gestalt inclination) and the phenomenological figure. The experiment is a field intervention practice that is used to explore this process. Perls spoke about using "the contextual method of argument" (Perls et al., 1973, p. 290), which means that the experiment consists in bringing out the context (the field) in which the person experiences his or her problem. In IGP, we do this by addressing the relationships that the person is a part of (exterior plural) and their meaning (interior plural) as well as the context in which thoughts, emotions, and motives (interior singular) interact with bio-body processes and action (exterior singular) and incorporating them into the current IGP work taking place in the here and now. *This involves bringing out the four quadrant perspectives.*

The meaning of the phrase *contextual method of argument* might best be understood if we look at an example.

If a person has a very clear conviction about something, even if this conviction does not match the objective realities very well, normal rational counter-arguments against his conviction might simply activate the person's defences. Instead, by taking an interest in and acknowledging the original thoughts and emotions (perceptions) that formed the basis, in the given context, for the development of the person's conviction, one offers the person a better opportunity for revising his conviction himself, on a new basis. The argumentation method lies in the actual uncovering of the *original* factual context (field), where the conviction was formed and made sense.

When we use *the contextual method of argument* in IGP, it acknowledges that what is perceived (especially in some therapeutic traditions) as defences and resistance in the person (the client) reflects the person's effort to care for his or her own conviction and, thus, care for his or her autonomy. In parallel with the general example above, this *conviction* can be characterised as the personal *theory*. In this context, the point is to acknowledge that even "wrong" personal theories were formed as a creative process and must have served an important purpose and had a function in terms of solving an important problem for the person (Perls, 1972, p. 291).

In the concrete IGP work, the practitioner can use the current context to explore a pattern in the person, facilitated by the following introduction: "You mention that in relation to other people you have this particular behaviour when you experience rejection. I suggest that we (both of us) pay special attention to how and when that shows up here, in our contact, in order to get a better understanding and per-haps discover something new about this pattern." Or the practitioner might address a contextual pattern that the person presents and bring it out in the here-and-now situation in order to explore it and learn more about it, as in this example: "You mention that you have this particular behaviour in relation to your mother. Let's explore it by letting you have a dialogue with her here and now. Try to imagine your mother sitting in that chair, speak directly to her about it, and then swap places in order to carry on the dialogue."

The purpose of the experiment, essentially, is that by exploring the context of the problem, the person discovers something new about its function. The point is that the person has acquired a gestalt inclina-tion that—although it may appear to be maladaptive—has served, and continues to serve, a purpose in relation to avoiding something else. Another point is that it can often be necessary to *experience* and iden-tify with this function in order to be able to change the gestalt incli-nation. That is, when you have experienced the original function of a problem or symptom, you will have a better chance of dis-identifying with it and reintegrating its components anew. Coherence therapy states that the function of a symptom should be experienced on a so-called pro-symptom level, where the pro-symptom position means the position where one has a direct experience of the emotional truth (or reality) in the symptom (Ecker & Hulley, 2007; Ecker & Toomey, 2008). From a neurological point of view, access to this pro-symptom level implies addressing non-verbal material in the limbic system in a manner where language alone does not suffice (Burley & Freier, 2004).

Neurons in the brain do not distinguish between reality and imag-ination, and, hence, the imagined experience of being present in the situation can activate unconscious "things" in the limbic system

(Kreiman et al., 2000). Thus, the experience can facilitate contact between the limbic system and the neocortex (Ecker & Toomey, 2008). In IGP, we use experiments to create here-and-now experiences of there-and-then events as a basis for working on the pro-symptom level, which, in our terminology, means working with (or virtually being one with) the experience of one's procedural gestalt inclination in order to allow one to dis-identify with its maladaptive aspects.

Good errors and bad errors: the meaning of radix

Gestalt psychologists distinguished very tellingly between what they called "'good' and 'bad' errors":

> ... the distinction between "good" and "bad" errors, which is promi-
> nent in Gestalt writings on productive thinking, was also there in
> Köhler's experimental work on intelligence in anthropoid apes (1925).
> A good error is one that somehow is appropriate to the structure of
> the problem situation, while a bad one is blind to it. ... The argument
> [concerning Köhler's studies of apes] is that pushing a box is a critical
> part of the solution. This simply isn't right: It's getting the box to be
> in the right place that's crucial, in terms of the radix of the problem.
> (Sharps & Wertheimer, 2000, p. 321)

Similarly, one can say that the person, with his or her organismic self-regulation in the past context (which was stored as a procedural gestalt inclination), solved an essential problem by means of what is, in the present perspective, a "good error"—good because it "solved" the essential problem and, thus, can be viewed as meaningful in the given original context.

According to gestalt psychologists, good errors are errors that are connected to the crucial core of the problem, that is, they relate to the potential solution of the problem, even if they fail to produce the right answer. The gestalt psychologists referred to the crucial core of the problem as *radix*, the Greek word for "root". The common feature of bad errors is to be blind to the radix (that is, the root of the problem).

This distinction, between, on the one hand, the radix, understood as the elementary level of the problem, and, on the other hand, what is indifferent or superficial in relation to the fundamental dynamics of the problem, is essential for feeling one's way to the core of a person's gestalt dynamics. Thus, it also affects how one chooses to initiate an experiment (and, essentially, how one chooses to focus one's aware-ness). For example, the practitioner must assess when the person's expression of anger helps to solve the essential problem, and when it is instead a response to an intervention that is blind to the person's fundamental problem (see the example on p. 44).

The purpose of the gestalt experiment is to support the person in his or her effort to achieve optimal (or healthy) organismic self-regu-lation. Optimal organismic self-regulation (as defined on p. 55) may be understood as situationally adequate self-regulation that is open to the future and free of the past. This form of self-regulation will func-tion most optimally in situations that contain an optimal degree of realism in the matching of direct perception and the construction of meaning. Organismic self-regulation takes place in the field on the contact boundary between organism and environment, and, as we have described, our perceptual gestalt process is a function of the field as such. It is, therefore, only possible to understand human behaviour if one knows the person's situation or context.

The capacity for understanding a given behaviour is specific to the context and the domain. In relation to the quadrant model then, opti-mal organismic self-regulation requires a mutual relatedness among the four quadrant perspectives. This means that the construction of meaning (left-side quadrants) in what can be perceived (right-side quadrants) must be optimally reality attuned, and that the individ-ual's behaviour and construction of meaning (upper quadrants) should similarly be reality attuned in relation to conditions and requirements in a systems and cultural context (lower quadrants). In IGP, we refer to this optimal reality attunement as *quadrant balancing*.

IGP is an experimental approach with multiple techniques

Traditionally, the gestalt approach has been seen as far removed from the academic scientific community. Paradoxically, this distance is virtually non-existent when/if the *experiment* is acknowledged as the basic method of the approach, as is the case in IGP. The point is that applying a scientific method of analysis and research in consideration of a field concept of health requires a research approach that does not, as a result of its own inherent premises, in itself pose an obstacle to uncovering potential complex conditions and relations in a variable and interacting field. That requires an approach that is both open and domain specific, and which incorporates phenomenological methodology. Furthermore, it requires an action-orientated research approach or other forms of *Real World Research* (Robson, 2011), which acknowledge the connection between the observing and the observed (that is, the fact that the researcher is also "of the field").

The IGP experiment should, thus, not be seen as synonymous with a set of techniques. The key is the use of experiments—as in experimental psychology—to test a hypothesis. An experiment, thus, includes focused attention on a given phenomenon with the purpose of confirming or rejecting a hypothesis.

A wide variety of tools can be used in this process. In the same way as the dedicated psychologist can take a methodologically pluralist approach, the IGP practitioner has creative licence (Spagnuolo Lobb & Amendt-Lyon, 2003). Hence, the design of an IGP experiment, or the range of techniques available to the IGP practitioner, is not restricted by pre-determined methods. It is the practitioner's ethically disciplined creativity that defines the limit to possible experiments. However, with inspiration from Clarkson and Mackewn (1993, pp. 98–99), we can outline certain general guidelines for sequences in the experiment:

1. The experiment should address something that is of immediate interest to the person, and which the person has brought up him/herself.
2. The IGP practitioner proposes (or designs in cooperation with the person) an experiment, understood as a context where the person can explore the field and increase his or her awareness, irrespective of the outcome.
3. The IGP practitioner can help enhance the focus (awareness) on the gestalt dynamics, for example, by inviting the person to exaggerate/amplify or inhibit his or her present behaviour.
4. As the contact with suppressed/denied behaviours or emotions outside the person's awareness (which are located in the implicit and procedural memory systems) grows stronger, the person's "excitement/anxiety arousal" increases. The person will experience what Perls calls "the Impasse", which will have a certain degree of similarity with the creative point of indifference and

with the undifferentiated field. It may also be perceived as an existential crisis where the person is stuck between excitement and fear, corresponding to what is known as the pro-symptom position in coherence therapy.

5. The experimenting space is a safe emergency space where suppressed emotions and behaviours can be allowed to be fully present in the person's awareness and produce a new figure–ground formation, which may alter the person's experience of his or her I-boundaries.

6. The person accepts the new figure–ground gestalt formation (which, through identification and dis-identification, has integrated and transcended the former gestalt dynamics) as his or her own. This produces a sense of "this is me feeling, thinking, and doing this" (other-ness has become I-ness and can, therefore, now be contained by the person's own I-boundaries).

The guidelines for the IGP experiment capture the fact that the process moves from something that is immediately present in the person's perceptual field (UL) to something that unfolds in one or more of the other quadrant perspectives. As mentioned earlier, this process involves testing (or exploring) a hypothesis. To illustrate this, we can look at the example of the neglected child (p. 77) who "solves" the unbearable life situation by means of a gestalt formation that has been stored as a procedural gestalt inclination, one that defines him/herself as the problem rather than the parents' behaviour. This child has had good reasons for adopting this gestalt inclination, and it is deeply embedded in the adult person's procedural memory as a reflection of a personal conviction or a personal theory.

Instead of attempting to change personal convictions and thoughts, the IGP practitioner, in cooperation with the person, designs an experiment aimed at investigating how the person's gestalt inclination is evident and what are its function, origins, and current (or lacking) usefulness. In a sense, the core of the matter is that the person—with or without being aware of it—operates on the basis of the assumption, or hypothesis, that the procedural gestalt inclination that he or she carries is useful and meaningful. The purpose of the experiment, then, is to test this hypothesis or theory and its value or usefulness in the person's gestalt inclination.

Only rarely is the person aware of his or her hypothesis or personal theory. The gestalt inclination is embedded in the person's procedural memory (for example, manifested in the body) and is typically only brought to the person's awareness as a result of the IGP process and the IGP experiment. This often brings out alternative gestalt possibilities that are more useful, with assistance from the IGP practitioner or, sometimes, spontaneously as a result of the person's own insight. In this context, "useful" means that they are more situationally adequate and contemporary as well as more suited for meeting the individual's intrinsic needs and, thus, also for creating a better flow in the organismic self-regulation.

The span of the IGP experiment

An IGP experiment can include almost anything that concerns the person's phenomenological reality in relation to the field that he or she has been a part of. The following are just a few examples.

- It could involve a focused conversation with the IGP practitioner that offers the contact opportunity that has been lacking in the person's life.
- It might involve an empty chair dialogue with someone else in the person's life, or an empty chair dialogue with a non-integrated aspect of the person (an aspect that is perceived more as other-ness than I-ness).
- It might involve encouraging and supporting an expression in the person that has not been unfolded, for example, by means of movement or tone of voice.
- It could involve the reconstruction of an original family structure in the form of a family set-up with the purpose of uncovering acquired restrictive gestalt patterns.
- It could also involve the use of structured or manualised interventions, provided they are used in the service of the person's phenomenological investigation of his or her procedural gestalt inclination aimed at developing optimal organismic self-regulation.

The IGP experiment, thus, aims at creating an opportunity for working with the person here and now in the person's context, as viewed from the four quadrant perspectives, even if the original context (the plural perspectives) is not necessarily physically present. In many cases, it is not possible to bring the physical context into the current reality: for example, when working with the person's relationship with a deceased family member. However, imagining (by means of "role-playing" or "two-chair work") *being* this late family member can be just as effective as if the other person had actually been present. Even if we work with the contextual argumentation method, where we bring the field into the current situation, the main focus is essentially on the person's *phenomenological field* in the practical IGP work. In the dialogue with a late family member, it is the person's experience of (and unfinished gestalts in relation to) the family member we are addressing, but by "being" the other person (and, so to speak, experiencing the person from within, in a *looking as* perspective) the person will usually be able to correct and expand his or her own phenomenology with these other field perspectives. Thus, the experiment is a way of bringing more of the field into the current situation. The following example will illustrate one possible way of doing this.

EXAMPLE

Person:	"I am so angry I could just explode over the way my boss treats me."
IGP practitioner:	"How do you manage not to explode?" (The practitioner wants to bring awareness to the person's way of regulating his energy.)
Person:	"I can feel the anger here, in my stomach, and then my shoulders tense up, and I grit my teeth. Yes, now I can feel the tension."
IGP practitioner:	"Imagine that your boss is sitting in that chair across from you." (An empty chair is placed across from the person. Instead of continuing to "talk about" the context, it is brought into the present.) "What is happening inside you right now, as he's sitting across from you?"
Person:	"Yes, now I can clearly feel, first the anger and then the way I tense up." (Sharpens his awareness of his bodily reactions and, in turn, his reaction to this reaction.)

"Right now it feels as if it's actually my dad sitting there." (The person spontaneously directs his attention to a reaction pattern from the history of the field that is activated in his relationship with the boss).

IGP practitioner: "OK, so put your dad in the chair instead. Try to follow your anger impulse." (Supports a natural flow from sensation to clarity to energy mobilisation to action.)

Person: (to the empty chair) "I hate the way you humiliate me." (To sharpen the emotion as figure—the step from sensation to clarity—the practitioner can support the person's expression, for example, by asking him to repeat the sentence or encouraging him to say sentences that begin with "I hate you for . . ." or by asking him to express the anger physically, for example by striking out. It is an important point, here, that this part of the process is not aimed at encouraging aggressive behaviour, but specifically at investigating the origins of the anger. Is it perhaps a secondary emotion in relation to an original sense of hurt?)

IGP practitioner: "Now sit in the other chair. Imagine that you are your dad, and also imagine that you are still sitting where you were sitting. What is your name when you are being your dad, and what is your response to what you hear your son saying?" (Switching chairs facilitates the shift in perspective and makes it possible for the person to see himself in a *looking at* perspective from the father's point of view.)

Person: (as his father) "I am surprised but also pleased that you are telling me this. And I've never told you how much I love you. I have had difficulty showing my emotions, and when you were younger I was so preoccupied with my own worries because of my business, and therefore I was too hard on you. I never really saw that until now, although I might have actually known it." (By experiencing the father's position in a *looking as* perspective, the person discovers new aspects that might help to loosen the fixed gestalt inclination.)

The IGP practitioner now asks the person to switch back to his first seat and continue a dialogue that promotes a reintegration of the polarised perspectives. It is the dialogue between the taking of the different perspectives that creates the contact and triggers the change. In this example, the dialogue brings the person into contact with the sadness and sense of rejection that the anger had covered up. Thus, this was a case of reactive, rather than proactive, aggression (see the discussion on p. 42), and the change required that the anger was identified not just cognitively, but experientially, in order to be dis-identified and later reintegrated in a more proactive form.

Summary of the fundamental concepts in IGP

So far, we have looked at the field concept in the systematic quadrant framework, we have investigated organismic self-regulation, gestalt dynamics, contact, awareness, and the gestalt experiment. The goal of IGP work is to incorporate the complexity we believe is required to overcome dual and seemingly contradictory conditions. To this end, we apply the systematic quadrant approach to describe field relations in relation to human life processes, which enables us to understand these processes holistically.

The gestalt process largely follows certain natural principles. We do not fragment reality arbitrarily, based on "the eye of the beholder". Our perceptual capacity is fundamentally developed to be able to perceive certain natural regularities in the objective reality. Thus, when we use gestalt formation to construct meaning and value, that process is not independent of factors in the objective reality, but always takes place in a certain perspective that influences which sections of the field we direct our awareness to and form gestalts in relation to. What we see and relate to in this process is figure–ground connections, which themselves form figures out of the larger contexts of which they are a part. Every gestalt is always part of a larger whole and contains other gestalts, which it transcends, includes, and inte-grates, corresponding to the concepts of the holon and the holarchy.

In addition to the quadrant-analytical approach to the study of complexity in gestalt formation, there are also contemplative ways that incorporate awareness training, meditation, and energy work. These ways of working with oneself and others reveal that the actual field relations are often more circular and interactive than one would normally be able to perceive. This highlights the fact that even the most thorough quadrant analysis of a gestalt process will typically be incomplete in relation to what one might discover via contemplation and meditation. The point is that both psychological analysis and contemplation are meaningful in our efforts to uncover and understand gestalt processes in the organism–environmental field analytically and to accessing contact with the total, undifferentiated field and the gestalt formation processes in the field. Analytical and contemplative approaches are complementary options in the effort to address complementary and holistic features and perspectives in people's lives. We say more about this in Appendix I, on awareness training and exercises.

In the following chapters, we take a closer look at various forms of IGP interventions and offer additional examples of IGP practice.

CHAPTER FIVE

Intervention practice

The scope of IGP intervention

An IGP practitioner has a holistic outlook and may, in principle, intervene in relation to any aspect and on any level of the field. This may involve interventions on an individual, group, or organisational level in the form of therapy, supervision, coaching, and organisational development. It could involve individual work with the inclusion of meditation, bodywork, and awareness training as part of an effort to break free from any maladaptive procedural gestalt patterns. It could involve work with couples and groups, where dialogue exercises and witnessing each other's honesty produce renewed openness to a developing co-existence. It might also involve educational and organisational work, where the quadrant schema is used to address the participants' understanding of the holistic perspective in the relationship between behaviour (upper-right) and meaning (upper-left) in systems (lower-right) and the cultural environment (lower-left) to help develop the capacity for perspective taking and help them understand how *meaningful disagreement* generates development with room for diversity.

The term *integrative gestalt practice* emphasises that it is not the domain or level of intervention (for instance, therapeutically) that characterises IGP interventions, but, rather, the approach as such. Drawing on the quadrant model, these interventions will rely on integrative field analyses as a basis for investigating how the gestalt process takes place.

It is awareness of the gestalt process that brings relevant change initiatives to light, and, in many cases, the uncovering of the process in itself triggers change. The paradox that the uncovering of field relations (and, thus, gestalt dynamics in the field) is often, in itself, enough to trigger change matches our earlier reflections on the self-organising character of the field and the consequent implication that the field, in itself, offers access to uncovering the dysfunctionalities included in it. To repeat Beisser's dictum, this reflects the paradox that "Change occurs when one becomes what he is, not when he tries to become what he is not" (Beisser, 1971). IGP intervention on any level rests above all on an acknowledgement of *what is*.

The gestalt process that takes place in the present includes the subtle shifts and avoidance movements in the person's awareness flow, including the ways that the person has developed to avoid feeling *what is*, and that cause pain (what we call "lumps" in the self-regulation wave). The IGP practitioner will address these avoidance moves (contact regulations or self-regulation mechanisms) because avoiding contact with the aspects of life that involve pain and suffering also means avoiding contact with other ("positive") aspects of life as it *is*. The intention is to bring the person into contact with his or her life and life management, including the aspects that he or she avoids being in contact with. In this effort, the IGP practitioner will use the quadrant model as the horizon for his or her special focus of awareness. That is the topic we shall now explore.

The quadrant schema as an awareness tool

The human inclination to form gestalts in figure–ground is associated with the basic human search for meaning. We generally find it difficult to stay very long in the open ambiguity that lies in maintaining that the figure in "Rubin's vase" simultaneously is and is not a vase or two faces (see p. 71), a place of ambiguity that is referred to as *the creative indifference*.

In the effort to help a person who presents a concrete issue, or perhaps merely a collection of fragments, it is a challenge for the IGP practitioner to avoid getting caught up by the content of what the other is talking about. That typically leads to searching for a particular meaning with the goal of identifying problem-solving behaviour, in part because one is motivated by a desire to help the other person as much as possible. A common problem here, however, is that the person who seeks assistance is stuck (fixed gestalt formation) in his or her attempt at arriving at a meaningful figure–ground formation and caught up in a narrative framed by a figure–ground formation created on a basis that is limited or far removed from reality.

The content (the person's narrative or story) can be viewed as a holon in its own right that is holarchically embedded in the more inclusive holon that constitutes the person's gestalt dynamics. How things are said (voice patterns, speech cadence, voice tone, and volume, syntax, verbal stereotypes, etc.), organismic expressions (posture, behaviour, eye contact, etc.), what is left out, and any patterns of contact avoidance (confluence, introjection, projection, retroflection, and deflection) are important openings that offer access to insight into the person's gestalt process and gestalt dynamics.

The point is not to ignore the content of what the person says, but, rather, to listen for other (and often more subtle) aspects in what the person says. The narrative content is part of a greater whole, which is initially unknown to the practitioner, and which is best uncovered if the practitioner adopts an openness that helps a new potential figure–ground formation to emerge. At the same time, in order to achieve an optimal understanding of the person's gestalt process, one should attempt to adopt the stance that all figure–ground formations that emerge are equally valid.

The fundamental IGP stance is not to see the person as a problem to be solved, but, rather, as a *sunset* to be taken in (Zinker, 1977). In enjoying a sunset, one would not, for example, suggest that the sun should be moved a little to the left to be just right, and neither would one be focused on figuring out what to do to make that happen.

> Look at the person the way you would look at a sunset or at mountains. Take in what you see with pleasure. Take in the person for his own sake. After all, you would do that with the sunset also. Chances are you wouldn't say, 'This sunset should be more purple' or 'These mountains should be taller in the center.' You would simply gaze with wonder. So it is with another person. I look without saying, 'His skin

should be more pink' or 'His hair should be shorter.' The person is. (Zinker, 1977, p. 22)

If one similarly—as Joseph Zinker also suggests—regards the person with a sense of *grandfatherly love*, one discovers that there is nothing that is wrong, nothing that needs fixing, and one maintains an affectionately interested curiosity about this existence and its way of functioning as a whole (Figure 16).

Upper-left quadrant perspective

In the upper-left quadrant perspective, the IGP practitioner empathises with the other person's situation in order to understand and

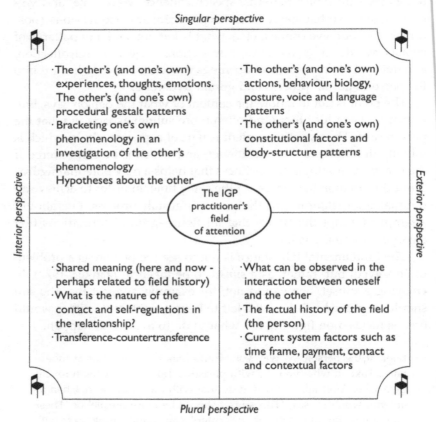

Figure 16. The IGP practitioner's focus.

bring awareness to the person's gestalt process. This involves "inclusion" (see Buber, 1937): putting oneself in the other's place, corresponding to a *looking as* position that, in addition to the awareness of the other's perspective taking as such, involves being aware of the other's self-perception. Adopting a *looking as* position requires "epoché", or "bracketing", which means suspending one's prejudices and preconceived notions to empathise as closely as possible with the other's experiential sphere. This is not about pre-existing knowledge, but about being open to learning something new about the client. This stance can be captured in the following statement: "You know too much if what you think you know prevents you from learning what you might learn by bracketing your preconceptions and being open to the other's experience" (Falk, 2010, p. 55, translated for this edition).

The challenge is for the IGP practitioner to use his or her own experiential horizon selectively in the service of therapy in order to promote contactfulness and uncover what might be hindering or inhibiting contact. Thus, the practitioner should not suppress his or her own experiences, thoughts, and emotions, but use them in an authentic, selective, and deliberately therapeutic manner. In a sense, *the IGP practitioner, with disciplined naivety, says what he thinks but does not say everything that he thinks.*

The fundamental and central healing focus in the upper-left quadrant perspective is on awareness. This is where the IGP practitioner can explore and facilitate the unfolding of the person's psychological life space, that is, the person's experience of the field as a whole. It is also in the upper-left quadrant perspective that the IGP practitioner can develop an understanding of the relationship between the person's current experience (thoughts/emotions) and his or her procedural gestalt inclination.

EXAMPLE

The person presents with symptoms of anxiety. Through phenomenological enquiry, the IGP practitioner facilitates a shared attention to the content and implications of the word "anxiety" for the person: having a stomach ache, having worrying thoughts about the future and the fact that the symptoms emerged in connection with the husband's infidelity a few months ago. By bringing awareness to these interacting aspects that make up the person's foreground, she gets into contact with childhood experiences of rejection and anxiety about the future. Her contact with the practitioner and the very act of sharing experiences that she had been keeping to herself have a healing function. Awareness of the old gestalt inclination that was embedded as a holon from a previous level makes it easier for her to accept the experiences of pain and rejection that life holds.

Upper-right quadrant perspective

In the upper-right quadrant perspective, the IGP practitioner will pay attention to where and how shifts and disruptions occur in the person's flow of awareness in order to enhance both parties' understanding of the organising structural aspects of the processes that are taking place here and now. When we see or sense the often subtle signs of disruptions or lumps in the natural energy flow (see the self-regulation wave (Figure 11)), and draw the person's attention to them, we can help the person get into contact with aspects and avoidance strategies that he or she is not in full contact with.

It is in this perspective that we see, for example, the tiny twitch by the left eye that, when it is simply brought into the person's awareness, makes the person burst into tears (that had been held back). The key is to have a present and focused attention on the person's body and behaviour and on the person's way of using his or her senses and contact functions (speech, voice, language, listening capacity, and other aspects of the sensory system), actions, disrupted actions, movements, etc.

These are a few examples of the IGP practitioner's attention to *form* in the person's voice. What is the pitch of the voice? How does the voice sound? Is it plaintive, threatening, inviting, shrill, etc.? Does the person reach you with his voice, or does he only reach half-way, so that you have to work extra hard to be able to hear him? Or is it rather as if he is speaking to someone who is further away, so that you almost feel blasted by his voice? What is the timing and rhythm like? Does he talk without pause, without giving himself a chance to listen? What stands out if one ignores the content and simply listens to the melody of the voice?

It is often necessary to make the person "slow down". Giving emotions the necessary time and space to link up with speech typically requires a slower pace. Some people use speech to disrupt or avoid contact with their own flow of awareness. Even if it might seem impolite or disrespectful to interrupt another person's speech, it could be exactly what is needed to help the person gain better contact with him/herself because it disrupts the person's (speech-based) interruption of him/herself. Situations where speech is used to generate narratives that prevent the person from being in the present and limit the person's gestalt flexibility are called "mind-y" in acceptance and commitment therapy (ACT) (Wilson, 2008). These are narratives that lack an embodied organismic quality. In traditional gestalt terminology, Perls distinguished, with his colourful words, between three forms of mind-y speech: *chicken shit* (chitchat), *bull shit* (intellectualisation), and *elephant shit* (philosophising).

In addition to the form aspect of the person's voice, the IGP practitioner will also focus on *form in the person's use of language*. This could involve the following. What is the syntax like? Does the person tend to negate what he just said with a "but . . ."? Perls suggested that one might ignore anything the person said before he says "but", since this "but" has already negated it. A variation on this is the person who, regardless of what the helpful practitioner brings up, replies with a "Yeah, but . . ." Does the person use jargon and irony, and what message does that hold? Irony and humour often have a deflecting function in terms of avoiding more direct contact. Is the same topic repeated again and again? Does it seem that there is something the person is not saying or is avoiding addressing?

The person's willingness to make eye contact is also a relevant focal point. Does he look down, avoiding contact? The practitioner may take a curious and inquisitive stance in relation to the role and function of the use of sight in the person's gestalt patterns. Sometimes, one may encounter a person with a gaze that is almost too open and contactful, which, in fact, serves as an attempt at confluence, or a person with a very direct stare, which might be another way of defending oneself from, or avoiding, contact.

Based on the figure–ground dynamics, the person's current behaviour and actions can also be seen as "figure" in relation to the body-structural "ground"—just as we posit a figure–ground relationship between the person's current emotions/thoughts and procedural gestalt inclination.

The way in which the procedural gestalt inclination has stored and manifests itself in the body constitutes the person's *body structure*. Although the organism always self-regulates to adapt to the circumstances as creatively as possible, these creative adaptation possibilities—considering the child's upbringing—have been limited not only by exterior conditions, but also by the organism's (biological and neurological) possibilities at a given stage of development. For example, for the child to use his or her muscles to manifest a "no" is only a real possibility once the child has reached a certain level of muscle development. Until then, the potential regulation in relation to "refusing" is limited to the regulation of gaze contact, protests in the form of crying/screaming, and mental "non-existence". Categories of possible ways for a child to self-regulate at the various stages of body development might have manifested themselves in the adult person's body structure, and the IGP practitioner may attend to the presentation of this body-structural background (as a fundamental way of being in the world) in the figure–ground or process–structure relationship in the upper-right quadrant.

Upper right is also where one can notice the person's constitutional physical factors, including any somatic diseases and somatisation symptoms, somatic factors (for example, obvious obesity), and basic existential body-conditions. There might also be specific somatic diseases, or somatic symptoms, that stem from conditions that are best understood in one or more of the other quadrant perspectives: for example, elevated blood pressure as a result of systems conditions such as a heavy workload (lower-right) and the person's gestalt inclination (upper-left) with regard to taking on excessive responsibilities. In relation to both psychosomatic symptoms and somatic symptoms in general, it is relevant to be curious about how these may relate to elements in the other perspectives, and what a dialogue among these perspectives might reveal in respect of this issue.

In relation to the *two lower quadrants*, the IGP practitioner attentively and respectfully explores the person's relationship with border and boundary (see Definition Box 3).

Lower-right quadrant perspective

In the lower-right quadrant perspective, the practitioner will attend to what is happening in the interaction between herself and the other. How are the two seated in relation to each other? How is the temperature and the light in the room? What is the connection between response and counter-response between the two? What was the link between what the IGP practitioner just said or did and the person's subsequent reaction? In addition, attention in the lower-right quadrant perspective will be aimed at the person's exterior contextual conditions: for example, economy, work conditions, family relations, and all the other interpersonal interactions that the person is a part of.

It is also in this perspective that we find family constellations in the person's history. For example, the person's mother might have been born during the Second World War in an occupied country as the result of an encounter between her mother and an enemy soldier. That is a lower-right factor that might have formed the basis of a family culture characterised by shame and secrets (which then concerns historical aspects in the lower-left quadrant). Or the situation could—as in the following example—revolve around an adopted child's acknowledgement of his or her field history background as the basis of achieving liberation as an adult.

> A young female client who was adopted when she was three years old says, in an aside about her adoptive mother, that had she not been her mother she is probably not the sort of person the girl would ever had had any contact with. The IGP practitioner draws the girl's attention to the fact that even though she calls the woman "mother", there is also a factual lower-right quadrant perspective reality where there exists a different (biological) mother. It proves to be important to articulate this fact as part of the girl's liberation from an implicit shared understanding in her adoptive family (lower-left quadrant perspective) which denies the part of the girl's history that was prior to the time of adoption.

Lower-left quadrant perspective

As illustrated in the example above, it is important to capture or explore the meaning dimension (in the lower-left quadrant) of what the person unfolds as events in the lower-right quadrant. The IGP practitioner should be open to the possibility that the meaning dimension might differ from the one that initially (perhaps supported by the person's own distorted image) seems most likely. Often, this perspective will uncover aspects that are new to the person him/herself, and which might be crucial for the person's ability to revise his or her self-narrative (life story, according to McAdams, 1993).

In the relationship between the IGP practitioner and the person he or she works with, the *experience of* "contact" is the most crucial feature in this quadrant perspective. We have previously offered a definition of the concept of contact based on the four perspectives (see p. 87), which made it clear that it includes an experiential side (upper left), a physical–biological side (upper right), a system fit (lower right), and a cultural character of being more or less appropriate to how we "contact" each other as a community (lower left). The individual's experience (upper left) of contact is hard to describe, precisely because it is experiential, but a key factor is the feeling of "being seen", which implies an open and non-judgemental, non-categorising attitude in the person who "sees". In this sense, it becomes a vitalising, meaning-making relationship (lower left) that constitutes a shared experience of contact. Therefore, the IGP practitioner's attention to all the other aspects, in both this and the other quadrant perspectives, should form a meaningful whole rather than disturbing the contact.

With reference to attachment theory, it can be understood as follows. From a very young age, we have the ability to perceive wholes and develop a sense of non-verbal signals (such as eye contact, facial expressions, tone of voice, body language, gestures, timing, and intensity). At one point, the child also begins to ask "why", which involves logic and concrete causality thinking. The development of a narrative self-domain (Stern, 1985), which forms the basis of the later development of life narratives (Habermas & Bluck, 2000), requires that the capacities for *perceiving* and *explaining* are brought together in an integrative form. A life narrative contains aspects of causal logic, but to serve as a meaningful narrative it must also integrate affects and autobiographical memory material. This gives rise to a certain narrative tone (McAdams, 1993), which affects the development of the life narrative in a more or less optimistic or pessimistic direction. The basis of the narrative tone is established in connection with the development of early attachment patterns (McAdams, 1993). This is also where the basis for the later emerging integration processes is formed as *secure attachment* (Siegel, 1999).

To the extent that therapeutic relationships function as attachment relationships, they may, in relation to persons with insecure attachment, serve to re-establish and enhance the person's ability to form integrative life narratives. While everybody tells stories all the time, one of the goals of therapeutic IGP work is to enable the stories that a person tells (his narratives) to be anchored and rooted in his lived body and experience. In extension of this point, the work involves combining the technical therapy work with acknowledgement of the fact that it has a healing effect for a person to experience how interesting he actually is (Polster, 1987).

The meaning dimensions of the unfolding of contact (lower left) in IGP work include, among other aspects:

- the existential meeting of two or more people;
- a working alliance between the parties;
- possible aspects of transference–countertransference in the relationship;
- certain meaning dimensions in the relationship (idealisation, devaluation, etc.) and the role of self-regulation mechanisms in the contact;
- taken together, it should be a vitalising experience in relation to the person's basic needs (for autonomy, relatedness, competence, and meaning).

An eye for whole and radix

What makes quadrant attention a challenging affair is the need to direct one's attention to the multiple facets of what happens in the relationship, based on the four perspectives, with the purpose of discovering gestalt patterns without having this emphasis overshadow or disturb the possibility of being in contact with the person or persons with whom one works. The key is to be able to have this awareness without identifying too closely with the purpose and without being swallowed up by the content of the person's story.

What, on the other hand, makes quadrant attention a simple affair is that, in principle, all that it requires is to be fully aware of what *is* rather than following the impulse to want to change or fix anything. Although this might sound simple, it is not necessarily easy, because we have an innate human inclination to want to solve problems, even if that might not be the most relevant angle in a given situation (Wilson, 2008). A therapist could, for instance, get caught up in the urge to solve the client's problem. This might be intensified by the therapist's desire to see herself as a competent therapist and by the client's expectation of having his or her problem solved. There could even be an insurance company involved that, based on evidence research, has calculated that it should be possible to treat a given issue (for example, anxiety) within a specific number of sessions. The therapist might have certain procedural patterns that promote or generate a feeling of never being good enough, which he or she might attempt to address by "getting results". Thus, there could be several "good reasons" for wanting to act as an "agent of change" and take on projects on behalf of the other person. It takes courage or patience to remain long enough in the creative point of indifference to gain insight into the operational logic that is at play in the person's organismic self-regulation.

By keeping an eye on the larger whole, the IGP practitioner improves the chance of discovering, together with the person, the self-organising character of the field and, thus, the person's gestalt dynamics. Having an eye for the *radix* means having a sense of the essential depth, or core, of the issue that is being addressed. The IGP practitioner will, thus, based on his or her sophisticated capacity for perspective taking, focus on both the function of the person's behaviour and the gestalt dynamics of that function (body reaction, emotion, thought, and action).

When a person's behaviour serves the *function* of avoiding a discomfort that is, in fact (in a right-side quadrant perspective), unavoidable, the behaviour will have only a temporary effect. The avoidance behaviour will perpetuate an avoidance pattern: it offers temporary gratification and, thus, motivates repetition (thus perpetuating the given gestalt pattern). However, because the avoidance behaviour deviates from one's deeper intrinsic needs, it will not be satisfactory in the long term. Furthermore, it typically activates a counter-reaction in one's body, senses, thoughts, and emotions that serves to perpetuate the pattern. For example: by side-stepping, I avoid the anxiety associated with engaging in a direct conflict with my co-worker (avoidance response). On the other hand, I can continue then to think that it is the other person who is a jerk (response to avoidance response). Thus, I face a double reactivity that might manifest itself as dialogues in my own mind, for example, the avoidance response to a potential conflict: "I want to turn down that assignment, but they would probably be disappointed . . ." and one's response to the avoidance response, ". . . but it could also prove to be an exciting challenge, so I'll grit my teeth and . . ." The avoidance behaviour, thus, activates a polarisation between inner voices that could restrict optimal organismic self-regulation, as reflected in the self-regulation wave with a reactive fluttering back and forth between overly inhibited and overly uninhibited self-regulation.

Because the inner voices have become polarised as a result of unmet intrinsic needs, the IGP practitioner might want to use the IGP experiment to facilitate an integration of the polar or complementary perspectives, for example, via a dialogue between the polarities (such as in two-chair work, see Kellogg, 2014).

By generally defusing the limiting thoughts, one can, to some extent, liberate energy for action, as is done within ACT (Hayes et al., 2003), but if defusing becomes a goal in itself, one risks losing contact with the value and the meaning that the specific and divergent, or polar, thoughts have, as seen from their respective perspectives. In IGP, therefore, we do not use defusion "as such" in relation to thoughts, but, instead, use defusion in relation to a principle of field complexity as a means of sharpening the individual perspective takings in their mutual dialogue in an effort to achieve integration on a higher level (see field theory and the metaphor of a brook running down a mountainside, p. 5). The purpose of defusion is to reach an understanding of the radix as the basis of transcending and including the diversity of inner voices (emotions, thoughts, needs, etc.) that have become positioned as fixed gestalt patterns and "unfinished business" in relation to the person's intrinsic needs and fundamental values.

When behaviour is viewed from the perspective of organismic self-regulation, a person's intrinsic needs and fundamental values will affect how the person self-regulates in contact with the environment. Feeling hungry is a *mundane* example, but it is also *elementary* and exemplary. Intrinsic needs and fundamental values are founded in the organism and also include the psychological needs for autonomy, competence, relatedness (see Deci & Ryan, 2000), and, one may add, the need to search for meaning in terms of something larger than, or beyond, oneself (Hansen, 2001a; Tønnesvang, 2012a; Tønnesvang & Hedegaard, 2014). In a horizontal perspective the organism self-regulates, but this regulation also takes place in a field that has a historical dimension, which implies a vertical regulation (see the concept of the holarchy, p. 2) in relation to the limited duration of life (see existential philosophy, Reflection Box 3, p. 34). The need for meaning, in its basic form, is related to the person's meaning making in relation to this vertical dimension. This corresponds to the point that the process of realising fundamental values and intrinsic needs does not take a linear course. While in a vertical dimension we strive to realise our fundamental values and needs, in a horizontal dimension we flutter back and forth between excessive and insufficient inhibition in our impulse control, a fluttering that is manifested in part as a mental activity in the form of inner dialogues.

If these inner dialogues are driven too much by the urge to avoid contact with what *is* and by *reactivity* to sensations, implying a short-term perspective, they might inhibit one's intentional stance in relation to needs and values. However, the dialogues will always be there—for better and worse—as an inescapable aspect of self-regulation.

EXAMPLE

I feel angry or unhappy about something that a co-worker does, but, because I am uncomfortable about engaging the conflict, I side-step (deflect). The dialogue in my mind might go as follows:

Voice no. 1:   "It's me. I'm being oversensitive and childish."

Voice no. 2:   "He's the one that's being completely unreasonable; you're just being a chicken when you fail to address the problem and tell him what you think."

Voice no. 1:   "We all have to get along; I'm sure he didn't mean it in a bad way. It's just his way of handling things."

Voice no. 2:   "Now you're bowing out again. In fact you know that it's just your conflict avoidance that's holding you back."

Voice no. 1:   "Yes, but at any rate it's too late now. It would seem ridiculous to bring it up at this point. If I was going to do it, I should have done it in the situation. But the next time it happens . . ."

Voice no. 2:   "Yes, you really should speak up the next time it happens."

The dialogue might actually lead to action the next time around, but, in many cases, the same dialogue is likely to come up again, since it worked fine as a warding-off technique: "I had an opportunity to address the situation internally and achieved a sense of reaching a resolution." The dialogue consists of two complementary inner voices and it can go on indefinitely, thus keeping the unexpressed emotion occupied. When we stick to our "shoulds", it feels a little as if we mentally act out the things we are afraid to act out (and, perhaps, should not act out) in real life.

ANOTHER EXAMPLE

In frustration over not having my way in my marriage, I blow up and slam the door. This may be a case of insufficient impulse control. As a possible reaction, I might later regret my outburst, and my inner dialogue might go as follows:

Voice no. 1:   "Damn, I did it again. I behave like a five-year-old. Am I ever going to grow up?"

Voice no. 2:   "I am totally entitled to let her know that I've had enough! She's being completely unreasonable. I want a divorce!"

Voice no. 1:   "It's just because I'm under so much stress right now—why do I need to take it out on her?"

Voice no. 2:   "But bloody hell, there has to be room for me too."

Both examples are about finding *situationally adequate, quadrant-attuned self-regulation*, and if they reflect typical gestalt patterns, they imply a procedural gestalt inclination outside the person's awareness. With reference to the self-regulation wave and the polarity between excessive or insufficient inhibition, both examples illustrate how a movement in one direction (manifested as voice no. 1) leads to a movement in the other direction (voice no. 2).

The quadrant schema as a methodological tool

The IGP practitioner may use a field-orientated approach focusing on specific aspects of the field, or a field-orientated approach explicitly applying the full quadrant perspective system. The IGP practitioner may also choose to restrict her attention to the person's relationships with the meaning of the history of the field in the dynamics of the current field. This would create a focus of attention that more or less matches the one found, for example, in certain recent psychodynamic approaches.

If, on the other hand, the IGP practitioner has a stronger focus on investigating and uncovering the mutual relations (lower right) and their meaning-making processes (lower left), the IGP practitioner's attention will match, for example, systemic thinking and intervention methods, framed by the field theory understanding that access to a solution of the problem is often found by uncovering the interacting positions and perspectives of the field (the system).

What, in general, characterises IGP practitioners' ways of navigating in different field dimensions is that they, with their awareness of working with methodological reductions, can (and will) be curious to learn more about how to generate insight and change as part of revealing a larger whole (the entire quadrant spectrum). However, the practitioner does not always use the quadrant model explicitly as a shared lens for viewing events together with the person. The quadrant model can also be used implicitly as an invisible matrix (in the back of the mind of the practitioner) for the practical IGP work. An advantage of using the model explicitly is that, over time, it will be stored as an orientation structure that generally helps sharpen the practitioner's awareness of the complexity of the field and reach to the core of the problem (the radix) more quickly and accurately.

The explicit use of the quadrant helps the person with whom the practitioner is working to develop a systematic cognitive mind map that facilitates that person's understanding of the gestalt process and the involved change processes. Although the model as a whole contains a high degree of complexity concerning human life processes, its basic structure is so simple that most people with normal cognitive functioning will not have any problem taking it in as a practical tool for grasping parts of their own field. This will, in turn, enable them to engage with the IGP intervention to develop a better understanding of their procedural gestalt patterns and gestalt inclination.

As one option, the practitioner could explain these aspects during the session by pointing out the various aspects that are brought to the person's attention. This may be done, for example, by writing keywords into a quadrant schema on a whiteboard, or by using a laminated quadrant schema to summarise the ongoing process. This explicit use of the quadrant schema can help the person differentiate the various quadrant perspectives in relation to his or her existential challenges and gestalt dynamics. In many cases, the people we have met in our IGP work have entered the process with some awareness of their "old patterns" and have been able to recognise them when they occur. That does not mean, however, that they have understood how the patterns were formed or how their own active roles were involved in perpetuating them, although they do know, on an intellectual level, that the patterns are not helpful. Having an intellectual understanding of one's patterns (on a semantic level of knowledge) does not, in itself, provide access to knowledge about how to change them (on a procedural level).

As already mentioned, there are many possible ways of using the quadrant model in practical IGP work. The following example (among many possible examples) will demonstrate how the model can be used, after a brief conversation, to summarise and anchor the person's cognitive insights in her gestalt process. In the example, the brackets refer to the quadrant perspectives.

EXAMPLE

The person: "I have this co-worker who is always criticising me. She always seems very stand-offish." (The person's experience is that another person seems stand-offish. At this point, we do not know what the co-worker did. Thus, so far the only knowledge we have relates to a part of the person's experience—"She is always criticising me" and "she always seems very stand-offish", an upper-left perspective—as it is described by the person. In order to understand the person's gestalt process we need to know more).

IGP practitioner: "In what way does she seem stand-offish?" (Invitation to unfold the person's phenomenology and promote the movement from the abstraction "stand-offish" to the actual gestalt process that produced the abstraction. This also marks a shift from the person's interior singular perspective experience (UL) of the situation to what the co-worker objectively did: lower-right perspective.)

The person: "She often looks away and begins to talk about something else when I try to contact her." (This is an observable act on the part of the co-worker, that is, from the LR perspective—incidentally, an act that might make up an observable aspect of the type of contact management that is characterised as "deflection".)

IGP practitioner: "What is happening right now as you're talking about it?" (Linking between awareness on what the person says in the UR perspective and the person's bodily/ emotional reaction in the present person in order to provide access to the organismic procedural patterns: parts of the structural aspect in the UL and UR perspectives.)

The person: "I am upset. I feel abandoned and not seen. It's like what my mother did when she had a migraine. Then she didn't have the energy to see me." (The person brings awareness to a historical field dimension and links awareness between the different quadrant perspectives in the past situation.)

IGP practitioner: "And what was your reaction then?" (Inviting a new potential integration of the perspective differentiations that were kept separate at the time. This is done by sharpening the person's awareness of how her organismic self-regulation took place there and then.)

Person: "At the time, I guess I thought that there must be something wrong with me—so I backed away, but I pretended that everything was OK . . . It's the same thing I'm doing now in relation to this co-worker. In fact I'm angry with her too, but I don't feel that I get to be angry . . . I want to say something to her, but I stop myself." (Here we see blocking or excessive inhibition in the self-regulation process between the stage that concerns clarity of the sensation and the subsequent stage, energy mobilisation, or possibly between energy mobilisation and action.)

As part of the summary, the practitioner now uses the quadrant schema together with the person (Figure 17):

IGP practitioner: "You tell me that your co-worker said—that was here (the IGP practitioner points to the lower-right quadrant), where the two of you were sitting in the office, talking, while what you felt was up here (points to the upper-left quadrant), and the experience you had in the contact with your co-worker (points to the lower-left quadrant), if I understand you correctly, brought you into contact with the mood that characterised your relationship with your mother back in your childhood (points to the lower-left quadrant), when she reacted the way you tell

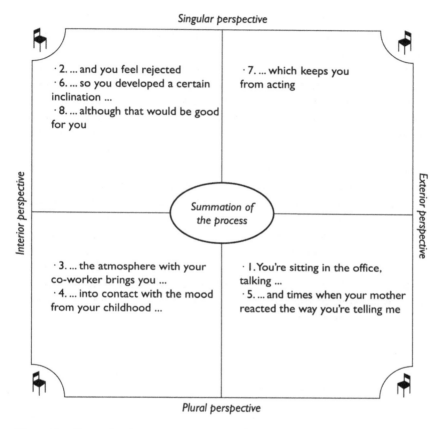

Singular perspective

· 2. ... and you feel rejected
· 6. ... so you developed a certain inclination ...
· 8. ... although that would be good for you

· 7. ... which keeps you from acting

Interior perspective

Summation of the process

Exterior perspective

· 3. ... the atmosphere with your co-worker brings you ...
· 4. ... into contact with the mood from your childhood ...

· 1. You're sitting in the office, talking ...
· 5. ... and times when your mother reacted the way you're telling me

Plural perspective

Figure 17. Example of quadrant summary of the process. The numbers 1–8 refer to the chronology of the process.

me she did (points to the lower-right quadrant). As I understand what you're saying, her reaction contributed to you developing this specific gestalt inclination or pattern (points to the upper-left quadrant), which keeps you from acting (points to the upper-right quadrant), even though that would probably be good for you. How does that sound to you?"

When the practitioner uses the schema in this sort of explicit effort to anchor the person's understanding of the process, the first part of the session often involves the practitioner plotting aspects from the various quadrant perspectives into the schema, sometimes together with the person. Later in the process, the two then work together to examine the connections that exist and are created among the quadrant perspectives.

In more intensive sequences, for example, in a therapy situation, where the explicit use of the schema might disrupt the contact, one, of course, avoids using it explicitly. However, in a summarising shared reflection on the aspects that were addressed, explicit use of the schema may add awareness and serve a summarising purpose. Often, a pattern will form with regard to connections among present issues, past factors, and procedural gestalt patterns, and it will, not least, help generate awareness of possible changes to these patterns.

The schema also becomes a tool that the person and the IGP practitioner can use together to take stock of the developmental process; filling out the schema continuously makes it possible to monitor any changes in the procedural organisation patterns: for example, as the person begins to behave in new ways or act differently in relationships. Thus, the quadrant perspectives make it possible to monitor the progression of the IGP process with a more general and shared holistic awareness of the unfolding processes.

The figure–ground relationship between here and now and there and then

Whether in the treatment of mental disorders or in self-development work, the IGP practitioner will attend to the field and the gestalt dynamics and, in each case, personal *development* will involve *dissolving* restrictions in one's gestalt inclination and gestalt flexibility. The task is to maintain a focus on the interacting quadrant aspects in the present while also focusing on the relationship between what is happening here and now (figure) and what happened there and then in the form of the history of the field (background).

Below, we offer an example of how the person might perceive and experience an interaction with the IGP practitioner (lower right) as a feeling of being rejected (lower left) with reference to a childhood situation (lower right) that was stored as a recurring experience of interactions with the parent (lower left) in the person's expectation and inclination (upper left), which often triggers a certain type of behaviour (upper right) in relation to others (lower right). In brackets, the example relates the process to the stages in the gestalt processes. The example stems from a previously published article (Tønnesvang et al., 2010, p. 589).

IGP practitioner:	"I notice that as I'm speaking, tears are welling up in your eyes." (With focused awareness the IGP practitioner invites the person to acknowledge sensation and emotion, that is, figure formation.)
Person:	"I can't take it any more." (The person seems to gain more contact with the emotions—the figure is sharpened.)
IGP practitioner:	"Look at me and say, 'I can't take it!'" (The IGP practitioner invites self/environmental scan and a deeper contact.)

The person looks at the IGP practitioner; her crying intensifies and goes deeper.

Person:	(*in tears*) "When you said that you had to cancel our next appointment because you had to attend a funeral, I felt as if you had stabbed me in the heart. I know it's crazy, but that's the way it felt. I almost ran away—I see now that that's what I normally do." (The person's awareness of old gestalt processes, which, over time, have become a structural aspect in the upper-left quadrant, becomes a new figure.)
IGP practitioner:	"Even with people you like and trust?" (The IGP practitioner invites her to sharpen the figure and, thus, promotes the person's movement from "identical with" to "identified with", or from a *looking as* position to a *looking at* position.)
Person:	"Yes, and I think I know where that comes from; it has to do with my mother's unreliability and persistent rejections. Eventually I withdrew completely." (The person experiences contact with the new figure.)
IGP practitioner:	"What do you do now that is different?" (The IGP practitioner invites her to sharpen the figure in a new gestalt process with better quadrant attunement.)
Person:	"I'm still here, I'm putting it into words, and I'm allowing myself to feel the pain." (The person confirms the sharpening of the figure.)

IGP practitioner: "Can you look at me and say that?" (The IGP practitioner invites the person to dwell on the new figure in her contact with the practitioner.)

Person: (looks at the IGP practitioner) "I am here."

IGP practitioner: "How does that feel?" (The person is invited to engage in contact with herself.)

Person: Scary but right." (Assimilation in the form of internalisation and integration.)

The example illustrates how the practitioner, by acknowledging and unfolding what *is*, facilitates a release from old procedural patterns and a potential gestalt formation that is liberated from these patterns.

For the practitioner, it is a matter of maintaining a defocused and flexible attention in all the quadrant perspectives in order to enable connections and parallels to emerge as figure. By defocused attention, we mean that one is not fused with the content in the various perspectives, and is, therefore, able to remain open to potential (also complementary) connections, even—and perhaps especially—if they seem contradictory or incompatible. This perceived incompatibility often reflects the fact that the practitioner's own pre-existing assumptions prevent him from discovering the complex field connections.

When a person presents a problem as having to do with anxiety, or depression, or stress, which are verbal abstractions of some specific experiences, there could be a risk that the practitioner forgets to investigate the factual aspects in the four quadrant perspectives because of his or her own pre-existing understanding of the respective diagnostic categories. As a result, one might think that one knows what one is dealing with, without actually determining, in relation to the quadrant perspectives, what lies behind the presented token of admission: "I am suffering from anxiety." Verbal abstractions and other ways of using language tend to bring us away from the present. In fact, it is often difficult for anxiety symptoms to persist once the person is brought completely into contact with the present: what are you feeling, in a concrete sense, in your body? What thoughts does that activate? Notice how your feet are in contact with the floor. Try to bring attention to your breathing, and so forth.

Although the IGP practitioner's focus is on the process here and now, this focus aims to uncover the structural aspects (inclinations) embedded in the processes in order to enable these to emerge as figure. The goal, then, is to uncover the gestalt inclinations in the "here-and-now" processes. The possibility of change is present when the procedural gestalt inclination forms the background of the figure that characterises the present gestalt process. In a sense, one works with a *double figure–ground relationship*, in part with the present figure–ground relationship and in part with the figure–ground relationship between the current gestalt (process) and the underlying gestalt inclination (structure).

In particular, the practitioner will focus on the person's way of disrupting his or her awareness flow. One might notice how the person is briefly emotionally affected and then rapidly changes the subject. It is these rifts, or shifts, that the practitioner will focus on and bring into the person's awareness. For example, "I sensed that something happened just there. It was as if you became a little emotional when you talked about your father." In many cases, such a comment might be enough to invite the person to dwell more on the emotion that he or she was rushing away from. This will enable the person to continue working on his avoidance patterns in order to help him be fully present with his emotions.

The contact is crucial, because the contact boundary is where the gestalt dynamics unfold. Generally, the IGP practitioner facilitates and encourages contactfulness by inviting the person or the group member to *speak directly to*, instead of *speaking about*, and by encouraging an expression of the emotions associated with the given contact. This applies both in the exchanges among the group members and, for example, in relation to an IGP experiment, where the person may be invited to speak *directly* to the imaginary person in the empty chair.

One may pay attention to whether the person's language supports contactfulness or the opposite: When a person consistently says "one" instead of "I", for example, it may suggest that she lacks contact with certain aspects of herself. In these cases, the practitioner might suggest the use of the word "I" to see whether that alters the person's experience. Focusing on contactfulness, as mentioned, involves investigating the person's contact regulations with a view to optimising them.

Examining the relationship between here-and-now gestalt processes and the procedural ground might involve uncovering aspects of the person's history (there and then) that could have influenced the formation of procedural patterns. The following example suggests how an IGP experiment can approximate a "re-establishment" of the context in which the person's gestalt inclination was formed, and how this re-establishment can be used to examine the contextual learning that took place at the time. The example illustrates how the person is encouraged to engage in contactfulness with the various field aspects of his experience of the original family dynamics.

EXAMPLE

The person presents his problematic relationship with women, which he somehow associates with his relationship with his mother.

The practitioner asks the person to pick persons among the other group members to represent the various family members from his original family (including a person who represents himself) and to place them physically in relation to each other in a way that reflects their mutual dynamics and relations at the time of the person's childhood that he associates with the problems he is addressing.

IGP practitioner: "Now stand behind the person representing your mother. Imagine that you are sensing your mother's existence as it was at the time . . . What is your name? . . . How old are you? . . . What is your life like? . . . What is your relationship with your husband, your children? . . . What would you like to say to each of them? etc. Say it to them directly . . . also say the things you're not saying." (Empathising with the existence of another family member also allows him to expand his sense of that person's organismic phenomenology. He is forced, so to speak, to apply an inside perspective on how it feels to be that person, cognitively, emotionally, and also in a purely bodily and sensorimotor sense—that is, from a *looking as* position.)

The person is asked to go on to the other "family members", going into *being* each of them and sensing the conditions of their existence, their thoughts, emotions, and actions from within. (This brings him into contact with each of the positions in the original family field and to sense the objective life conditions of these positions in right-quadrant perspectives and their phenomenology in left-quadrant perspectives—in a *looking as* position.)

IGP practitioner: "Now go back to your place, and look at everything from an outside perspective, from the place in your life where you are now . . . is there something that stands out to you?" (After uncovering field relations in the past, the person is now invited to examine the same aspect of the field from his current field perspective in a *looking at* position.)

Person: "I am noticing patterns and connections that I wasn't aware of before. I am able to understand her much better now. She felt very alone in this family. She never had my father's attention or love. She felt completely let down. I feel a strong sense of sympathy for my mother when I feel the powerlessness and the pain that she must have carried. I've never seen it that way before . . ." (Understanding his mother's position and actions provides access to forgiveness and care, which, in turn, leads to self-reconciliation and, thus, liberation from a procedural gestalt inclination that had caused the person to be unrealistically wary and suspicious of women in general. The change was driven by an uncovering of what is/was in the field as the person expanded his field of attention to include more field perspectives, both in the past field context and in the current field perspective. In addition, the process includes the following movement: from being identical with a particular attitude, he now identifies the real background, which we can also see as the radix of the problem, and he is finally able to dis-identify with the attitude, which marks a development on a procedural level.)

This new gestalt process is enabled by the person's awareness and acknowledgement of *what is*, or, rather, *what was*, in the original context but which, by virtue of the experiment, takes on the currency quality that activates the contact with the original gestalt dynamics.

In this case, this awareness includes the person's contact with the relevant family members' respective experiential perspectives in the original context and, thus, generates a new discovery in a lower-left quadrant perspective.

When awareness is brought to the field in the past, as in the experiment described above, it is, of course, the person's own *experience* of the field (his psychological field) that is activated. It begins with the experience or the story that he carried with him, but during the process it changes to another story. The family members' factual behaviour there and then (exterior plural quadrant) remain the same, but, by experiencing their positions and existence from within, the person altered the meaning dimension (lower-left quadrant perspective), which, in turn, altered the previous gestalt inclination (upper-left quadrants structural aspect).

The example illustrates that it is the actual uncovering of the complexity of the field that brings out new connections, enhances awareness and quadrant attunement, and promotes healing. Thus, we see how a re-presentation (see the etymology of the word: re-presence) of the person's phenomenal perception of reality of a field context in the past can be brought into the present. In addition, we see how this creates new openness to the future—that which Scharmer (2007) calls "presencing".

Subtle interaction and experience

As part of putting oneself in someone else's position (*looking as*) one strives to see the world and, thus, also oneself from the other person's perspective. At times that may involve, as in the example below, seeing oneself differently in this person's perspective than in one's own everyday perspective.

> *IGP practitioner*: "I understand that you feel that I am angry with you, and even though I have no knowledge of being angry with you, I am interested in knowing more about what it was I just did or said that make you feel that I am angry with you." (Although the person expresses that she has observed something that the IGP practitioner does not recognise, he does not reject it, but acknowledges the person's UL-perspective with a view to adding depth to the LR perspective. The practitioner might learn something new about himself (his own UL perspective).

As in the example above, the person might perceive the practitioner as being angry, even if the practitioner does not perceive himself as being angry. It is essentially impossible to determine whether one person or another is right. It is a meeting between two phenomenological realities, and being a professional does not mean that one knows everything about oneself, including whether one is signalling irritation or anger (and perhaps actually being angry on a subtle level) without being self-reflectively aware of it. It also does not make sense to assume simply that the other person is projecting. The practitioner could, in fact, be displaying anger without being aware of it. Whether or not that is the case, it might be more important to stay with the person's experience, since it is, after all, the person's gestalt dynamics one is seeking to understand rather than determining who is right. Whether one is the practitioner or the client, one is not always in immediate contact with the more subtle aspects of what is going on inside. We will come back to the differentiation between awareness and bodywareness (pre-reflective awareness) in the next section.

A person's experience includes thoughts and emotions and is anchored in the body. The IGP practitioner will be focused on preserving the explorative openness together with the person, even when experiences occur that are not fully integrated into the person's cognitive phenomenology. While body therapists, as a key part of their approach, manipulate the body in order to achieve psychological impacts and change (see, e.g., Lowen, 1977), the IGP practitioner's focus will revolve instead around a constant curiosity about how bodily and psychological aspects in this particular person constitute perspectives on the organismic whole. The IGP practitioner will seek to support the person's autonomy by helping the person discover, from his or her own perspective, body sensations, and their meaning rather than using body therapy interventions to trigger change. The IGP practitioner may bring attention to the somatic symptom and be curious about its function; for example, the practitioner may ask the person to try to identify with and imagine *being* his or her symptom in order to make something that is implicit in the person's existence more explicit with a view to facilitating a better integration of meaningful aspects of meaning. This method is also found in *externalisation*, as it is called in narrative therapy (see, e.g., White, 2006).

EXAMPLE

IGP practitioner: "Now imagine that you *are* your headache. What is your existence as a headache like? And what do you, as a headache, do to the person who has you? Try to talk to her."

Person:	(*as the headache, speaking to the person*) "I am strong and persistent, and I want your attention . . ."
IGP practitioner:	"Now be yourself again, and answer the headache, and then try to continue the dialogue by switching back and forth so that you identify with whichever one of you is speaking."
Person:	(*as herself, speaking to the headache*)"I hate you—I just want you gone."
Person:	(*as the headache*) "I am stronger than you, and I want more room."
IGP practitioner:	"You want to claim more room . . . Try to expand, headache, and take all the room you want . . . and you, the one who is having the headache, try to allow it to fill you out completely."
Person:	"The pain is growing less intense . : . The headache is telling me that I need to claim more room in my life than I normally do, and that I need to allow myself to take charge more . . ."
IGP practitioner:	"It sounds as if you have a body signal that you can listen to when you neglect yourself?"

The organismic understanding makes the IGP practitioner fundamentally curious about understanding somatic symptoms in a broader field concept based on quadrant perspectives. Somatic symptoms often serve as a link to subcortical cerebral layers and our procedural memory. The "language" of the implicit memory is also the body's language (upper-right quadrant perspective). The practitioner might ask, "What are you feeling right now?" "What are you aware of right now?" and "What are you feeling in your body right now?" But also, for example, "What would your backache say to you right now, if it could speak?" Somatic aspects and symptoms are part of the body whole. The parts are aspects of the field and part of the gestalt or the holon that we call the "organism". By identifying with the different aspects (meaning, experiencing them from the inside as a subject), we can expand our contact with our phenomenological field and integrate pre-reflexive awareness in our cognitive phenomenology. Symptoms can also often be seen as an expression of existential pain in a more general sense. A symptom might prove to be related to certain contexts (the lower quadrants)—for example, the person who always develops a headache when the mother-in-law comes to visit. We are familiar with expressions such as "she's a pain in the neck", "that problem is his headache now", "a weight has been lifted off my shoulders", "he was smothered by her love"; or "being stiff-necked", etc. These expressions illustrate how somatic concepts are used as *Metaphors We Live By* (Lakoff & Johnson, 1980).

We should emphasise here that this is not about psychologising somatic diseases that require medical treatment, but about being curious, together with the client, and seeking to discover links between physical symptoms and interacting aspects that can be discovered from the other quadrant perspectives.

"Bodily" aspects

Our language contains a fundamental dichotomy that is typically expressed as, "There's me—and there's my body." We do not have an everyday word for the *body-self*. We are more likely to say that we *have* a body than that we *are* a body. We tend to think that the entity that *has* this body resides in the mind. When mental performances and cognitive capacity are given precedence, as is generally the case in western culture, the body is reduced to a sort of physical appendage to the mental.

Part of the reason for this distinction between me and my body might be that one can handle bodily perceived pain by separating "oneself" from one's body. This is most pronounced in traumatised individuals, for example, victims of incest, who, by dissociating from the violation of the body ("this is not happening to me—it only affects my body"), handle the abuse by means of this sort of organismic (divisive) self-regulation. In the given context, this self-regulation may, in fact, be the most meaningful—in some cases the only—way to survive with one's self intact. Other incidents of pain and suffering in life that the organism encounters as a natural part of being alive in this world may also be managed by dissociating from the bodily reaction, which lets us avoid sensing the full and true drama of life. The consequence of these dissociation processes is an inability to identify with what has been dissociated and, thus, also an inability to dis-identify with it, which restricts our development.

In accordance with Kepner (2001, p. 39), we base IGP-work on the fundamental understanding:

1. That any psychological/existential theme that a person presents is part of a larger whole (gestalt/holon), which also includes body aspects.
2. That any bodily expression, for example, a somatic symptom that a person presents, is part of a larger whole (gestalt/holon), which includes psychological, existential, and contextual aspects.

Precisely because body and psyche are commonly dichotomised, the IGP practitioner will attempt to create a certain atmosphere that facilitates and provides access to experiences of the underlying unity of body and psyche. This suggests the need to work at a somewhat slower pace than is generally common in relation to mental issues. It also requires helping the person to experience the bodily nuances "from within", so to speak. The IGP practitioner might, especially if he wants to facilitate the person's contact with what the bodily dimension has to add to the understanding of the field ("the embodied field"), for example, approach it as in the following case.

EXAMPLE

IGP practitioner: "I see that you are leaning forward slightly, resting your right hand on your stomach." (Brings awareness to what is immediately observable, UR.)

The person nods affirmatively.

IGP practitioner: "Is it all right if I just try that position myself?" (Respect-fully requests the person's permission, supports contact-fulness, and enables the dialogue to move into "the embodied field" that encourages pre-reflective body-wareness.)

Person: "That's OK."

IGP practitioner: (adopts the same position) "Is this it?"

Person: "I think my hand on my stomach is a little higher up— closer to the solar plexus."

IGP practitioner: "Thanks for correcting me there. Now I can feel the difference that it makes. I can tell that it is a little harder for me to breathe when I lean forward like this, and that my hand sort of protects my stomach. Is this what it feels like for you?" (Mirrors the person by testing his body phenomenology and asks for feedback on the mirroring.)

Person: "Yes, and now I notice that I feel this sense of emptiness in my stomach . . ."

IGP practitioner: "You say emptiness. Could you try to describe exactly what that feels like from the inside? What is the body sensation that makes you call it emptiness?" (Helps bring differentiated awareness to the bodily processes that have led to the person's abstraction/conclusion: "emptiness".)

Person: "I feel pain."

IGP practitioner: "When you say pain—is it a stabbing pain or more of a throbbing pain?" (Helps the person find and differentiate between words that are close to body sensations.)

Person: "It's the feeling I had as a kid when I was sitting alone in my room . . . when I had withdrawn in anger and was hoping that someone would come in to see me." (Here we see an anger that covers up a sense of vulnerability and pain that formed the primary emotion. This primary emotion can be invited out more with continued work on the bodywareness level, as it is embodied.)

To the extent that the person's words and language are the result of the gestalt process that the person is carrying out, it also marks an abstraction from (or *interpretation* of) processes, which, incidentally, also unfold in the body. However, if the person's words and language and, thus, abstraction from the experience seem plausible to the IGP practitioner, because the practitioner engages in the same sort of abstractions or interpretations, there is a risk that the process will fail to uncover the organismic process that led to the abstractions inherent in the words and the language. Classic examples of this are when a therapist thinks that he knows what a person means by "being depressed", or "having anxiety". It is always necessary to uncover what the term implies more specifically to the person one is working with. Or, if one sees tears welling up in the person's eyes and says, "I can see that you are upset," when, in fact, the tears might relate to many other ways of being emotional. With his comments, the practitioner risks making the person interpret (form a gestalt of) his or her response as sadness. A more open-ended comment would be, "I can see that there are tears in your eyes now."

In the example above, we see how the practitioner avoids assuming that they have a shared understanding of the term "emptiness". This lets them explore the details and the dynamics of the experience of the term "emptiness" for this particular person. We also see how the IGP practitioner can address the relationship between pre-reflective and reflective aspects of awareness. The words we use to describe our body sensations often reflect the *end result* of the many nuances and processes in the body experiences. When we want to go to the core (the radix) of the person's procedural gestalt inclination, our aim is to uncover the micro-processes with their organismic foundation.

This endeavour is made more difficult by the fact that we often lack words that are sufficiently close to the body sensations to describe micro-processes with an organismic foundation. As illustrated in the example, by tuning in (*looking as*) and testing the person's posture and body sensations on his own body, the IGP practitioner may help the person find the words that describe the body sensations most adequately. When the IGP practitioner, towards the end of the example, makes suggestions as to whether the pain is stabbing or throbbing, rather than simply asking the person what sort of pain it is, he does this to help the person "stay with the body" and feel what is happening there rather than "moving into the mind" to search for the right word. Thus, it might be helpful for the IGP practitioner to try to use words that help the person "stay with the body" so that the gestalt process can unfold from here. This could involve working with metaphors for the function of the symptoms as a way of providing access to flexibility in the gestalt dynamics, but when the person takes over the practitioner's metaphors (which are also verbal abstractions), there is a risk that the new gestalt process is generated more by the practitioner's interpretation and gestalt inclination than by the person's "creative indifference". In Ryan and Deci's (2000) terminology, this corresponds to the person acting from a controlled self position rather than being self-determined. A rich discussion of how various therapy forms promote, respectively, exterior, controlled, or autonomous self-regulation is found in Ryan and colleagues (2011).

Having a body focus does not mean neglecting the content of what the person brings out or the associations this might produce. It simply means that one may switch between treating the body and the body processes as figure and background, respectively, in relation to what is being discussed. Further, when one returns to treating the body aspect as figure, one may *in-corporate* the other aspects (psychological, existential, contextual) that were brought up, for example, by returning to the question, "What are you feeling in your body right now, after we have been working on your relationship with your father?"

As mentioned in an earlier example, during one's upbringing one will be prepared, metaphorically speaking, to "kill parts of oneself" as part of one's creative adaptation in order to survive. This is very much about avoiding feeling and sensing in order to limit the experience of pain. When the IGP process is aimed at bringing the body "to life" and returning to the full use of all one's senses, it also involves feeling the pain that one has sought to avoid.

Viewed in a quadrant perspective, we are dealing with a less healthy state when there is a split between a person's perceived notion (upper-left quadrant perspective) and the person's body sensation (upper-right) of the environment. This split is most extreme in people with schizophrenia and in schizoid conditions, but it is also common for people who do not fully "reside" in their body and who seek to dull their senses in a variety of ways in order to avoid suffering. Living fully, however, involves feeling the pain and suffering that are also part of life, without dissociating. In the words of Polster (1987), gestalt work can be seen as bringing the drama back into one's life.

On therapy, supervision, coaching, and leader development

The IGP practitioner's interventions are aimed at influencing procedural/structural patterns in one or more quadrant perspectives with a view to bringing about enduring changes.

Therapy and supervision

In therapy, the practitioner has licence, so to speak, to intervene on an intrapsychic or psychodynamic level (upper-left quadrant perspective), which is not quite the case in supervision and coaching. In the therapy setting, the quadrant perspectives, in a sense, mainly facilitate work that—based on the client's perceived problem—takes place in the upper-left quadrant. "In and down" is how some would character-ise the direction that characterises psychotherapy, and one might add, "in and down into the analysis of the procedural gestalt dynamics".

In supervision, on the other hand, the direction is much more "up and out", in the sense that the work with the supervisee's action potential (right-side quadrants) *may* include the acknowledgement of procedural patterns in an interior singular perspective without, however, addressing them on a deeper therapeutic level. Instead, one will focus on the individual's actions in the field, which is the person's work-based reality. Thus, supervising an individual in an organisation involves focusing on the individual's behaviour in the organisation while considering the factual individual aspects (both upper-quadrant perspectives) as well as the factual organisational aspects (both lower-quadrant perspectives).

In group supervision, the quadrant model offers a common third to which all the participants can relate. For example, if the supervisees are all from the same workplace, the model can help remind them how there might be different individual experiences and perspectives on reality (upper-left and lower-left quadrant perspectives) among the participants, although the organisational and objective exterior factors (exterior plural perspective) are the same. In that case, the quadrant model helps the participants differentiate typical right–wrong dichotomies that hamper well-being and developmental processes in the workplace.

As mentioned earlier, the quadrant perspectives form a lens that can be applied regardless of whatever structures and methods the supervisor uses otherwise. Supervision techniques such as "reflecting team" and "reflecting processes" (see, e.g., Andersen, 1991) are ways of expanding the field that is addressed in the supervision space. A reflecting team makes it possible to contribute other people's field perspectives (from the lower quadrants) on the supervisee's and the supervisor's shared meaning-making. These structures can, thus, be meaningful to include in the context of IGP supervision.

With its quadrant perspective, which is free of content, IGP super-vision generally offers an open and integrative approach to various supervision forms (schools) and their methods. Here the various schools will be viewed as approaches that contribute partial truths about processes and drivers of change. Similarly, the methods of the various approaches will be seen as partial methods that might offer valuable tools in relation to various issues. The IGP approach is, there-fore, also a natural element in supervision groups, where the partici-pants are trained in a variety of theoretical and therapeutic formats. The IGP approach implies an open-minded attitude to the various perspectives and respect for their particular ways of accessing reality. Some approaches prototypically see things in an exterior plural perspective, others in an interior singular perspective, and so forth. The art is to make the various contributions engage in *meaningful disagreements* with each other in establishing the most flexible (and coherent) basis for creating change and positive development. The quadrant model in particular can help accomplish this.

Leader development and executive coaching

Coaching the leader of an organisation can offer an indirect way of also working with the part of the field that the leader is in charge of, that is, the organisation—and its development. Working with the organisation by coaching the leader is an example of what we referred to as a methodic reduction of the field in the first part of the book. Even while working on an individual footing with the leader, one is still aware of the broader field, the organisation, which is influenced by the coaching process, and that offers a way of working indirectly with the organisation as well. As one manager who undertook an IGP process commented, "The fact that I have worked personally with my old patterns and the way I act in relationships has had a huge effect on improving the culture in my company. For example, we have become really good at celebrating our victories together after I had learnt to acknowledge and celebrate my own victories in life."

The leader's way of leading, including his personal "blind spots", is crucial for the operation of the company (lower right). In creating transformational visions and ways (Bass & Riggio, 2006), and in setting behavioural standards, the leader has a special impact on the corporate culture and the vitalising quality of the psychological oxygen in the company (lower left) (Tønnesvang & Nielsen, 2006). For example, employees often copy the leader's way of providing leader-ship. If the leader is conflict-avoidant and inclined to sweep conflicts under the rug, it will often be difficult for the staff to manage conflicts appropriately and effectively. This will devitalise the organisational milieu and probably also hamper performance and well-being.

As documented by Nohria and colleages (2008), among others, transparency in the organisation's management and decision-making processes is a key parameter in promoting employee commitment and positive attitudes towards the workplace. Viewed in the framework of the quadrant perspectives, transparency not only pertains to incentive structures (LR) but also affects the corporate culture and professional standards (LL) as well as the individual employee's commitment (UL) and actions (UR).

Some leaders will be aware to some extent of their own limitations (patterns) and the importance of "looking at" oneself. Many have, for example, carried out tests that indicate their "focus areas" on a personal level, but this often fails to lead to changes in their behaviour. Approaches that focus on the leader as a person, and which include tests for uncovering personality profiles and personality types, may give leaders intellectual insight into their own blind spots, but they do not necessarily give them the tools they need to change. Blind spots are generally related to what we refer to as the person's procedural gestalt inclination. For example, it is obviously meaningful for a leader to delegate tasks. There are models specifying stages in the delegation process, as described, for example, in situational leadership. Although the leader understands the importance and the value of these stepwise models, in our experience it is still often a challenge for the leader to delegate appropriately. Self-regulation patterns (lumps in the self-regulation wave) and, thus, patterns in the leader's own procedural gestalt inclination prevent the learning from being applied in a manner with an organismic foundation that is open to the future, free of the past, and situationally adequate.

Relating the self-regulation wave to the leader's energy management, for example, the leader might have difficulty maintaining a balanced energy flow when faced with confronting a conflict (an imbalance just before "action" or, perhaps, even earlier in the self-regulation process), or perhaps the leader has difficulty respecting his or her own organismic needs for rest and restitution (an imbalance in connection with "withdrawal"), or the issue might have to do with not being fully present and in contact with the staff. This might be due to a pattern of avoidance, or a tendency to save time by more or less skipping the "contact" phase).

Simply put, the self-regulation wave illustrates that one should pay attention to what it is one needs to do, and what the situation calls for, and then do it. The effort to identify and dis-identify with mal-adaptive gestalt patterns on the procedural level naturally addresses aspects that are traditionally included in other approaches, for exam-ple, situational leadership as well as assertion training, active listen-ing skills, prioritising, etc.

> Due to stress symptoms, the leader of a large treatment facility took part in an IGP course in personal development for leaders. As a future daily practice, he chose to use a brief breathing meditation exercise (described on p. 178). He has now used the exercise every morning for several years, followed by dwelling meditatively on a work-related topic or other organisational issues that pop up. The exercise helps him sharpen his focus on what is unfinished and what requires action, and it offers the restitution (withdrawal) that he needs to be able to act proactively from a personal base (sensation–clarity–mobilisation–action–contact with target–withdrawal) in his leadership. He has not had any stress symptoms since he embraced this practice. A disciplined practice such as this can help a person (possibly supplemented with coaching or therapy) to stay centred in relation to his or her own self-regulation.

To some, the theories in this book might seem complicated. In practical IGP work, however, it has been striking to observe how easily and immediately people who have never dealt with psychology and psychological theories intuitively understand that there is a connection between their inner sense of integrity (listening to and staying true to oneself) and their actions in accordance with this integrity (also with consideration for others). This is the essence of optimal organismic self-regulation, and it is the essence of balancing the four quadrant perspectives. As a leader said during a course, "Everything works optimally for me when my four quadrants are balanced, which also means that I act based on my own integrity." We could not have put it any better ourselves.

Intervention in organisations

Organisational work

When intervening as an IGP practitioner in a broader part of the field, as one does in organisational work, for example, the quadrant model is a useful tool for clarifying relations and issues. An organisation contains both individual members with their individual experiential horizons (interior singular), individual actions (exterior singular), mutual actions within the organisation's formal structures, hierarchies, and rules in the given societal and global reality (exterior plural), and a corporate culture (interior plural), which, in many cases, also includes a variety of subcultural aspects: for example, associated with individual departments, traditions, etc., as well as office politics and informal leadership structures.

There is a mutual dialectic influence between the organisation's structural (including management related) and cultural aspects, on the one hand, and the psychological and physical state in the people working in it, on the other hand.

The quadrant model can help uncover what we have previously described as the *radix*—the core of the problem—to avoid searching for solutions to the problem in the wrong quadrant perspective: for example, by individualising organisational shortcomings or issues that may, on closer analysis, prove to relate to management tasks. Thus, it reflects a lack of acknowledgement of the radix when a leader refuses to take on an unpleasant managerial responsibility such as carrying out necessary layoffs and instead hires consultants or supervisors and attempts to present the problem as anything other than a managerial task, for example, as communication problems internally among the employees. That represents avoidance behaviour.

A quadrant perspective on the organisation

When IGP practitioners use the quadrant model and the self-regulation wave as lenses in working with an organisation, they may be simultaneously aware of individual organismic processes in the organisation's individual members (upper perspectives) as well as systems/organisational (lower right) and anthropological (lower left) perspectives. They can switch between applying the quadrant perspective on the organisation as a whole, on the individual departments, or on other partial aspects, and on the individual members of the organisation.

While working with the organisation as the holon being explored, the practitioner may also, for example, have an eye for the leader or the leadership team as a holon and vary the holon focus on a continuous basis. The organisation is a holarchical structure, where the holon *organisation member* is part of the holon *department,* which is part of the holon *organisation,* which, in turn, is part of a larger context in *the total field.*

In this context, obviously, the IGP practitioner's attention to the micro-processes that are constituted by the individual's gestalt dynamics and procedural organisational capacities mainly serves as background for the practitioner's work, not as figure.

Occasionally, one may be faced with an assignment that the client wants solved as an intervention on one level, for example, individual coaching, but which, during the process, as field relations are uncovered, may change to make intervention on another level seem relevant. This might occur precisely because an uncovering of the field reveals it to be meaningful to intervene from a different quadrant perspective.

> An assignment began as individual coaching of a head of department who was on sick leave due to stress symptoms (UL and UR). He had been referred by the company's managing director. After a few conversations with the person, it became clear that certain key organisational (LR) issues were a strong contributing factor to his stress. This included unclear procedures and uncertainty about decision-making competences between the various levels of management—problems that seemed to be related to recent organisational changes. With the person's consent, the IGP practitioner contacted the managing director. Subsequently, they all three had a number of meetings where the decision was made to continue the process with a focus on the organisational structure.

The subsequent process, where the practitioner worked with the management team for a period, clarified what organisational changes (LR) were needed to optimise procedures. Thus, what began as an individual coaching process changed into a process aimed directly at a larger part of the field, the organisation, based on a LR-quadrant perspective.

In organisational work, the IGP practitioner may, for example, have organisational members (perhaps grouped according to their professions or departments) do group work where they share problems and developmental aspirations with each other and with management. This helps to clarify the experiences (LL) of the individual departments/professions (LR). In this process, the IGP practitioner can explain that the experience of problems (see the field theory) in

itself often contains access to solutions, and, hence, bringing the problems to the surface in a more explicit manner can be a constructive
way of creating change. At the same time, one may point out that,
since the experience of a problem is affected by one's vantage point, it
is essential to listen to all the perspectives in the organisation (persons,
departments, professions). When wishes and problems are then
presented in plenum, some of the aspects in the organisation that have
led a hidden and implicit life become open and explicit. That will be
a way of bringing out and identifying *what is*, but which is rarely
expressed or addressed so directly.

This process, in which the participants have their experience
acknowledged and are listened to, often has a healing effect in itself.
Furthermore, acknowledging *what is* (see the paradoxical theory of
change), will, in itself, already offer an opening for dis-identifying the
identified and, thus, trigger change and development. Making *what is*
present (re-present) in the here and now (as an IGP experiment) can
prevent dissociation in the development of the organisation and pave
the way for *presencing* the emergent moment (Scharmer, 2007).
Bringing attention to all four quadrant perspectives can lead to full
awareness in relation to the present and, thus, a greater capacity for
sensing and facing the emergent moment—the future. More generally,
this will focus attention on some of the things that need to be
addressed in the reinvention of organisations, as proposed by Laloux
(2014).

Presenting the quadrant model to the employees of an organisation makes it available as a common reference or an operating system
for development in the organisation. In the quadrant perspectives, one
can describe the movement from what was to what is and, further, to
what is the preferred future. It also offers a way of enhancing the
shared focus on determining in which quadrant to take the first step
in the process of change. Introducing the concepts of development *vs.*
dissociation further ensures a common understanding of the importance of qualified identification and dis-identification in relation to
organisational development, for example, by ensuring that the participants actually identify the experiences that are made, so that they can
be integrated in future initiatives. Figure 18 presents a model for
working with the relations between past, present, and future in the
four quadrant perspectives in organisational IGP work. Figure 19 is a
verification of the model posing questions to the past, the present, and

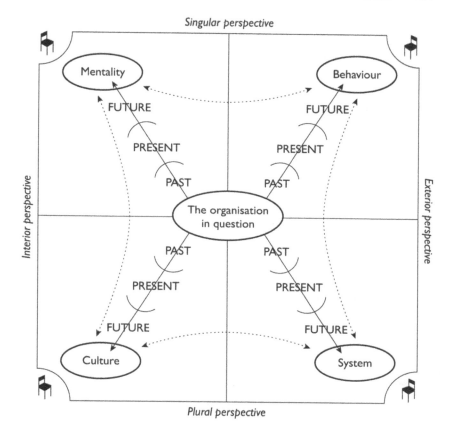

Figure 18. Integrative operating system for models about organisational development. The practitioner can use the quadrant model, together with the members of the organisation, to illustrate what the conditions were like in the organisation before, what they are like now, and what desires or expectations there are for the future. For example, in the lower two quadrants, one may note the organisational structure that was in place before and the one that is in place now after two departments have been merged into one. What are the concrete implications of the merger (LR), and how does it correlate with the changes that seem to have occurred seen from a lower-left perspective (for example, general resistance, dissatisfaction, and an observable increase in sick leave)? These conditions can also be examined in the light of the reactions of the individual members of the organisation (that is, from the two upper quadrants). The key is to discover how these experiences and analyses can be used in reflections on how best to implement the development of the future organisational structure. What sort of behaviour and mentality in the individual employees do they wish to promote? What sort of organisational culture do they wish to promote?

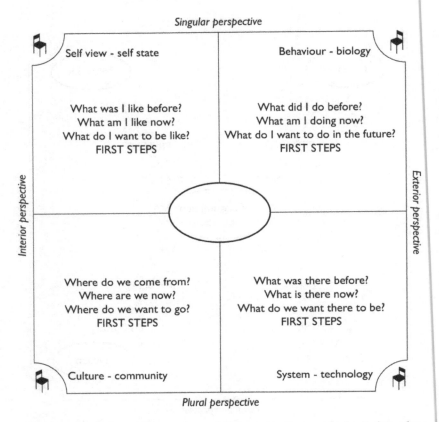

Singular perspective

Self view - self state

What was I like before?
What am I like now?
What do I want to be like?
FIRST STEPS

Behaviour - biology

What did I do before?
What am I doing now?
What do I want to do in the future?
FIRST STEPS

Interior perspective

Exterior perspective

Where do we come from?
Where are we now?
Where do we want to go?
FIRST STEPS

What was there before?
What is there now?
What do we want there to be?
FIRST STEPS

Culture - community

System - technology

Plural perspective

Figure 19. Work sheet. The members of the organisation can be invited to adopt a *looking as* perspective and take an active part in clarifying future goals for the organisation from the perspective of the four quadrants. The figure illustrates how important it is that considerations about where one wants to go are based on what is and on what was. The "first step" indicates the importance of moving beyond simply talking about things and embracing a concrete action orientation: What should happen next? Who should be involved in this? How, and in relation to what conditions (time span, optional/mandatory, etc.), should it be done?

the future in each quadrant. Figure 19 includes the action orientation, in that it also asks: what shall be the first step?

IGP as an art form: creative experimentation

The medical tradition distinguishes between the art of medicine and medical science, although the latter seems by now to have ousted the former. There is a risk that the same might happen, in the name of evidence-based research, in the field of psychology and psychother-apy. When we consider this a risk, it is not because we find it irrele-vant to study the efficacy of therapies, but, rather, because this is done in a manner that risks ignoring essential aspects of the complexity of psychotherapy.

IGP contains a wide diversity of methods and techniques that the experienced practitioner can use in addressing psychological issues and challenges. These methods and approaches include verbal and non-verbal techniques and experiments, sensory and awareness exer-cises and training, energy work, bodywork, voice work, the expres-sion of emotions, dream work, fantasy journeys, psychodrama, poetry, family reconstructions, modelling, drawing, music, movement, dance, etc.

To a large extent, IGP practice involves giving licence to profes-sional creativity. The effort to bring awareness to how individual persons—in the most creative ways—have adapted to their surround-ings throughout their life, developing adaptation patterns in the organismic regulation of contact, contains considerable opportunity in the practical IGP work for experimenting with this contact manage-ment in order to provide access to liberation from the limiting imprint of the past.

The practical IGP approach may have an experimental and playful character; "playful" in the sense that there are no general, pre-deter-mined rules for how therapy should unfold, for example. This is determined in the experiment, where the IGP practitioner and the person together—based on the person's phenomenology—explore the person's gestalt formation process in the organism–environmental field in order to discover new and feasible ways of developing more optimal and quadrant-attuned gestalt formations.

An IGP practitioner works in an emergent and ever-changing field, where the choice of techniques and interventions depends on the specific context and what the situation requires and calls for. Precisely how the IGP practitioner develops the expertise to master this process cannot be fully conveyed in a book. With an emphasis on the event character and the creative aspect of the practical work, one can claim that it is an *art form* (Zinker, 1977), which cannot be described in a manual, but which needs to be experienced to be understood properly. Indeed, like any other art form, IGP work is practised differently by different practitioners, just as any artist has his or her own "line". This is *not* a bias, as some evidence studies see it, but a crucial point in relation to the unique quality of the encounter with people, who are all unique.

In IGP, we have a positive focus on the importance of creativity and unpredictability in the socially emerging fields that arise in the meeting of people. In practical IGP work, we use different method tools to match professional creativity to the purpose of uncovering the procedural gestalt inclination as a field phenomenon in order to enable and facilitate change.

IGP can be practised in one-on-one approaches (for example, individual therapy or coaching), where the person's gestalt patterns, as previously mentioned, will be revealed in the interaction with the practitioner. There may, however, be certain advantages to working with IGP in a group setting, as awareness of the interaction among the group members offers a unique opportunity for addressing the organism–environmental self-regulation in interpersonal relations. Group work offers unique opportunities for experimenting with many structures and methods in the exploration of the individual's contact regulations in the organism–environmental field.

The other group members may serve a variety of functions in the work with the individual's organism–environmental contact. The group reflects the environmental (the others') perspective on the individual person (witnessing, feedback, etc.). The importance of the witnessing and feedback function of other group members is seen, for example, in cases where a participant, who has worked in an IGP session to liberate himself from a maladaptive procedural gestalt pattern, might feel a certain sense of insecurity about how other people will perceive him when he shows himself without this pattern. As an aspect of the previous procedural patterns, he might still have an expectation that he will be rejected by the others, or he might experience a sense of shame or embarrassment in connection with revealing more of his "true self".

Honest and appreciative feedback from the group members can play a crucial role. His "negative" expectations about how the world will perceive him when he expresses himself authentically, based on his own senses and emotions, are challenged, reality tested, and revised. This here-and-now reality testing and correction of the organism–environmental field promotes optimal organismic self-regulation (dissolution of lumps in the self-regulation wave and improved attunement among the quadrant perspectives).

The creative IGP practitioner can also, as shown in the example on p. 134, use the other group members in family reconstruction setups and other types of relational re-enactment aimed at bringing the original field context (from the historical dimension of the two lower quadrant perspectives) into the present for a phenomenological exploration of the field "there and then". It is, literally, the practitioner's professional creativity that sets the limit for the format of ethically justifiable IGP work. This licence to be creative is not a reflection of a laid-back or *laissez-faire* attitude, but of a deep-felt respect for the complexity and possibilities of human life when it is not limited by one-track logic and quick-fix, evidence-narrowed methodologies.

CHAPTER SIX

Discussion and perspectives

An integrative framework for psychology,
psychotherapy, and intervention

IGP is an integrative framework for a variety of ways of practising gestalt work. Furthermore, IGP is also integrative in relation to other forms of psychotherapy and intervention approaches, just as they, in turn, provide inspiration for IGP. In accordance with the notion that "no brain is smart enough to produce a 100% error" (Wilber, 2003), it is part of the fundamentals of IGP that *any theoretical approach to reality possesses validity from its own given perspective, provided it reflects an angle on reality.* IGP is, thus, focused on understanding how other approaches to the same issue can make their partial contributions to an ever more integrative IGP.

Existing gestalt therapy contains variations in practice (O'Leary, 2013). There are approaches that include a particular body focus (Kepner, 2001) in the phenomenological investigation and in therapy, a focus on cognitive phenomenology, an interest in the narrative aspect (Polster, 1987, 1995), a preference for experimentation (Zinker, 1977), family therapy (Kempler, 1981), a special focus on relational issues (Yontef & Jacobs, 2008), and a particular attention to contact disruptions (Hostrup, 2010) as well as a more field-orientated approach without this focus (Jacobs, 2011).

There are many other psychotherapy approaches, and many new approaches are emerging. Since Freud, *psychoanalytically orientated forms of psychotherapy* have moved towards an emphasis on relational and interpersonal issues, and gestalt therapy, too, has been described as a relational and psychodynamic form of psychotherapy (Hansen, 2001b). Psychoanalytic self-psychology, object relations theory, and interpersonal psychotherapy have moved in the direction that was Perls' original intention with the gestalt approach, which was to insti-gate a revision of Freud's psychoanalysis (see Perls, 1969) with regard to both focusing on relational aspects in the form of the contact between therapist and client and challenging the structural model of psychoanalysis. Recent psychodynamic psychotherapy points out the importance of affect in contrast to purely intellectual insight in the therapeutic process. Diener and colleagues (2004) have pointed out that affect-focused techniques have clear positive outcomes in psycho-dynamic psychotherapy. A number of approaches work systematically with affect as a key theme: affect phobia therapy (APT) (McCullough & Magill, 2009), emotion focused therapy (EFT) (Greenberg, 2002), mentalization-based therapy (Bateman & Fonagy, 2006), compassion focused therapy (CFT) (Gilbert, 2005), and varieties of intensive short-term dynamic psychotherapy (ISTDP) based on Habib Davanloo's method (Abbass et al., 2014). These approaches are largely in accor-dance with IGP's basic concept of the emotional experience—and not only analytical and cognitive insight—as an important factor in creat-ing new understanding. Furthermore, Clarkson (2011, p. 30) has pointed out, with reference to Conduit (1987), that techniques that appear to stem directly from the gestalt approach have successfully been incorporated into Davanloo's method.

Systemic therapy and *social constructionist approaches,* like IGP's field orientation, have their background in Lewin's field theory, where uncovering the interacting positions and perspectives of the field (the system) can serve as a key access point to solving problems. In IGP, we focus on the way in which gestalt formation and, especially, gestalt inclination form figure in relation to the background out of which it emerged.

To a large extent, the background consists of what has become the person's self-narrative. In *Every Person's Life Is Worth a Novel* (Polster,

1987), *A Population of Selves* (Polster, 1995), and other sources, Polster has addressed how the gestalt approach works with the client's "storyline", enabling the client to revise his or her self-narrative, as a parallel to different forms of *narrative therapy* (for example, Schafer, 1996; White, 2006).

As in cognitive–behavioural therapy, IGP also contains an analysis of the person's behaviour that includes the person's experience (thoughts and emotions). Traditionally, cognitive therapy has focused on restructuring thinking and changing behaviour (Tønnesvang et al., 2010), but, in recent years, that has changed radically, not least with what is characterised as the third wave of cognitive therapy, including acceptance and commitment therapy (ACT) (Harris, 2008; Hayes et al., 2003; Wilson, 2008), which considers it essential to acknowledge pain rather than seeking to eliminate it to gain access to change. This marks a parallel to the paradoxical theory of change (Beisser, 1971), as it is used in the gestalt approach. As previously mentioned, the concept of *mindfulness* in mindfulness based cognitive therapy (MBCT) (for example, Segal et al., 2002) is used in parallel with the awareness concept in the gestalt approach. Like gestalt therapy, ACT and RFT (relational frame theory) (Törneke, 2010) point out that when we fuse with the content of language and thinking, language and thinking keep us from being in contact with what is, because the inherent character of abstraction in language can cause a distortion of, and a phenomenological distance from, the immediate experience with its organismic foundation.

We see a clear parallel between the basic concept in ACT and gestalt therapy in the following statements: "Get out of your mind and into your life" (Hayes & Smith, 2005) and "Lose your mind and come to your senses" (Perls, 2006) or in statements concerning the self as a process: "The self is not to be understood as a fixed institution" (Perls et al., 1973) and, from ACT, "From a behavioral perspective, self is not a fixed entity" (Wilson, 2008).

With *transformational chairwork*, Kellogg (2014) has modified a manualised version of the "two-chair work" of the traditional gestalt experiment to a schema-based therapy. In IGP we can *both* acknowledge the value of these methodological refinements of the most effective elements in the gestalt approach *and* point out the risk of a fragmentation of the holistic understanding that characterises the gestalt approach and, thus, IGP.

In relation to the concepts of organismic phenomenology and bodywareness in IGP, it is also interesting to note how some of the current developments in MBCT include conceptual models (*interacting cognitive subsystems*—ICS) that seek to incorporate the crucial role of the bodily dimension, in the sense of the person's felt sense, for understanding the complexity of the behavioural and cognitive processes (Teasdale, 1999; Worsfold, 2009). Indeed, Teasdale notes that

> . . . it has come as no surprise from the ICS perspective that major recent importations into modified cognitive therapy have come from Gestalt therapy, which, like ICS, emphasises the importance of holistic levels of representation, the role of body state, and of the wider semantic context. (Teasdale, 1993, p. 353)

Coherence therapy, which we have referred to earlier in the book, points to factors that are also included in IGP. According to Toomey and Ecker (2007), the symptom is the person's psychological means of ensuring his well-being and cementing his security, as he has concluded, on a non-reflected psychological level, that the pain associated with the symptom is less than the pain that the symptom prevents him from experiencing. The symptom is, therefore, essentially meaningful and an expression of the person's (unconscious) inclination for self-protection. The symptom is seen as being unconsciously self-made by the person as a *necessary solution* to a particular existential dilemma (Ecker & Hulley, 1996, 2007; Toomey & Ecker, 2007)—cf. "the self-organising dynamics of the field" and "procedural gestalt inclination".

Toomey and Ecker say that

> Efficient symptom cessation stems from first having the person experience, inhabit, verbalize and embrace the emotional truth of the position that does have control over producing the symptom, his or her symptom-requiring prosymptom position. People are able to change a position they experience having, but are not able to change an unconscious position that they do not know they have. (Toomey & Ecker, 2007, p. 219)

In accordance with the paradoxical theory of change, coherence therapy holds that "complete acceptance and profound change are the same" (Ecker & Hulley, 2007, p. 5).

With its organismic approach, *somatic experiencing* (SE) harmonises well with the focus on the somatic aspect of the organismic phenomenology in the IGP approach—what we call bodywareness. The neuroaffective relational model (NARM) (Heller & LaPierre, 2012), which uses somatic mindfulness to enhance self-regulation in the nervous system, and which addresses the connection between the psychological and the somatic by promoting access to the body's self-regulating capacity, is a conceptual framework that makes good sense in an IGP perspective in the relationship between the two upper quadrant perspectives.

Like IGP (and with a more explicit focus), existential psychotherapy (Deurzen-Smith, 2012; Yalom, 1980) has a special focus on the meaning and consequences of the fundamental dilemmas associated with the human condition or the existentials (in the form of death and the issues of meaning, existential isolation, freedom, responsibility, and existential anxiety). As we describe in Reflection Box 3, we relate these dilemmas to a comparison of the exterior–interior quadrant perspectives in relation to the person's responsibility for his or her own life management.

Based on the field concept that everything is related, mutually affects each other, and is in constant motion (which implies that every moment is also a process moving towards a next moment), it is further interesting to focus on the degree to which it is possible to have or gain contact with this next (emerging) moment—that is, the future dimension of the field. To be able to speak of a process moving towards the coming moment is an implicit aspect of the field concept and the concept of awareness. One is always aware of something, and this something, in itself, contains the movement towards the next moment.

In a gestalt terminology, the process can be said to move from one figure–ground formation to the next, where the creative point of indifference is the transition phase from one to the other. Developing sensitivity to this phase involves gaining access to anticipating the coming (emerging) moment as well as developing awareness towards what the Buddhists call emptiness—in the sense of emptiness to any figure–ground configuration.

That is one of the aspects that Scharmer addresses in his "Theory U", under the term *presencing*, which describes a movement where one approaches one's innermost self *from the perspective of the future that is about to emerge* (Scharmer, 2009). The word *presencing*, according to Scharmer, involves *sensing* and *being present in the moment* (*presence*). It is a form of "emergence awareness" that is not only directed at the present existing whole, but at the very source that the arising, potential future will spring from. This emergence awareness might also be called a *radix awareness of the emergent field*.

According to Scharmer, we need—and are also beginning—to reach the deeper level of awareness that the presencing concept suggests. Theory U offers a language for speaking about this deeper level as well as a methodology that helps us operate from this new level of awareness where one is free of tendencies to repeat (download) past familiar patterns and, thus (in our terminology), approach a "situationally adequate, future-directed, and past-free gestalt inclination". A condition for sensing the emergent moment in the field is to have an open sensitivity to the incipient place in itself as a process.

In relation to IGP, Scharmer's concept of presencing can be said to capture the aspect of the moment that concerns an "*of* the field" emergence awareness of the undifferentiated field where the creative indifference provides access to sensing (being aware of) what the next figure–ground formation process might involve.

Applying the quadrant logic to Scharmer's presencing approach reveals that an "*in* the field" emergence awareness may occur in specific parts of the emergent field (see Figure 20). Thus, we can observe how a person may have, for example, a well-developed emergence awareness in relation to the development potential of organisational systems that does not necessarily involve a similar emergence awareness to one's own, as well as others', psychological growth and development potential. The quadrant model lets us differentiate four main foci for "*in* the field" emergence awareness, directed at, respectively, psychological, biological, systems aspects, and cultural aspects, corresponding to a distinction between psychological, biological, systems, and cultural emergence awareness.

IGP is both an organising framework and a practical approach for integrating parts of the complexity in the various forms of therapy and combining them. With their focus on particular perspectives, several of these new approaches help confirm certain aspects of the IGP approach and, thus, its general validity. Often, the new

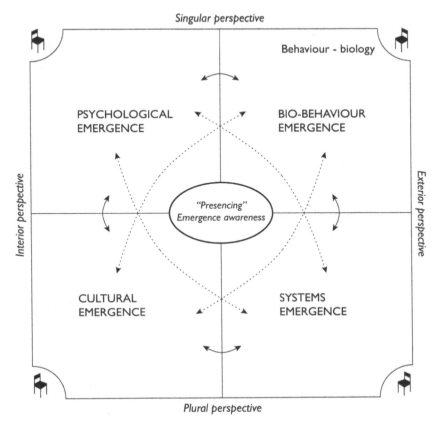

Figure 20. Quadrant differentiation of presencing. The figure shows a differentiation of four aspects of presencing corresponding to emergence awareness in relation to, respectively, psychological, biological, cultural, and systemic factors.

approaches (schools or methods) refer to a specific systematic frame-work, selected techniques, and a scheduled progression in the therapy process. The traditional gestalt approach has tended to encourage the therapist's own creativity and intuition more. In that perspective, there are advances from the new approaches that we can draw inspiration from and integrate into the integrative gestalt practice while also, on this basis, contributing to systematising partial insights into a more integrative holistic understanding of the phenomena we work with than the other approaches usually take into consideration.

Evidence, diagnostics, and intervention

Quantitative research methodology has its origins and its foundation in the right-side quadrant perspective, while qualitative research methodology is rooted in the left side of the quadrant model. Both are relevant. One should not exclude the other, since their goals differ, and a more adequate understanding requires both approaches (Black, 2008). This is quite in accordance with the point of view in the growing number of *mixed method* approaches in general psychological research (Tashakkori & Creswell, 2007; Tashakkori & Teddlie, 1998).

Examining the concept of evidence in relation to the effects of psychotherapy through a quadrant lens reveals that aspects of the holistic quadrant concept are rarely the subject of effect studies in typical evidence research. This has also been pointed out by Beutler (2009), who—without applying quadrant thinking—documents that evidence focused research oversimplifies the complex connections that psychotherapy addresses. The point is that it is mainly very specific therapeutic interventions and methods that can be described and controlled in a sufficient manner to warrant statements of any certainty about specific effects. Although it is not hard to find techniques in a gestalt approach that can be isolated and subjected to evidence studies—for example, "two-chair work"—the narrow basis that has so far been applied in evidence research means that it is difficult to measure and rate an approach such as IGP, in part because the specific methodological strategies that are used in IGP differ from situation to situation, depending on the character of these situations and the professional judgement of the IGP practitioner.

Given these reservations, if we nevertheless look at evidence-based studies of gestalt therapy, cognitive therapy, and cognitive–behavioural therapy, there are actually studies showing that gestalt therapy presents results that are at least as promising as the (more evidence-tested) cognitive approaches (Strümpfel, 2004). To recapitulate what we wrote in Tønnesvang and colleagues (2010), Beutler and colleagues (1991) found that gestalt therapy outperformed cognitive therapy in the treatment of depression. Johnson and Smith (1997) found that, in the treatment of phobias, the gestalt technique with the empty chair and cognitive desensitisation were equally effective in comparison with a non-treatment group, and that the gestalt group, unlike the desensitisation group, indicated a number of benefits that went beyond the specific focus of the therapy.

As also mentioned in Tønnesvang and co-authors (2010), Watson and Bedard (2006) compared forty clients who were classified as having either good or poor outcomes from cognitive–behavioural therapy and manualised gestalt therapy; the finding was that the good respondents in both therapy approaches showed a higher capacity for emotional processing, and that the clients who had received gestalt therapy wound up showing greater capacity for emotional processing than the ones who had received cognitive therapy.

Finally, we pointed to the classic comparative study by Johnson and Greenberg (1985) in which it was found that cognitive behavioural therapy and gestalt approaches are equally efficacious, and that there is a benefit in gestalt therapy that is not present in cognitive therapy, which is that the people who have received gestalt therapy continue to improve after the therapy has ended instead of merely preserving the progress they made in therapy. The latter point can be presumed to be a result of the focus in gestalt therapy on the level of the procedural memory.

In extension of this last point, Folensbee (2007) points out that sensory systems and the part of the memory that is embedded here are stimulated more by gestalt therapy than by approaches that focus more on intellectual analysis:

> By emphasising sensory systems, emotions, and direct connections to motor action, change is encouraged with less emphasis on the frontal, declarative systems than in other therapies. Primary integration centres seem likely to be highly active during Gestalt therapy experiences, while frontal/hippocampal declarative integration systems seem likely to be less active during intense experiences. Complex neural network patterns are presumed to be activated through implicit connections more than through declarative, explicit decision-making. The resolution of incongruence between declarative awareness and non-declarative, implicit processes is facilitated by Gestalt experiences in therapy. Integration of implicit and explicit processing is assumed to lead to the development of explicit decisions that are more effective because they incorporate implicit processing. (Folensbee, 2007, pp. 164–165)

It is this procedural inclination (embedded in the implicit memory) for performing and ascribing meaning to things in a particular way—the procedural gestalt inclination—that we seek to affect in IGP in our effort to promote change.

Diagnostics and intervention in relation to people's life management

The gestalt process diagnostic and the systematised field analysis (the quadrant model) offer a basis for developing a shared language and a shared understanding in relation to applied psychology and its theoretical foundations. It gives us a prognostic tool that includes all four field perspectives and will, therefore, contain psychological, somatic–neurophysiological and other interacting aspects seen in an anthropological, cultural, and socio-economic systems perspective.

From a quadrant perspective, one may examine the individual's gestalt processes and behaviour in the field, and the quadrant model lets us uncover the dynamic relationship among the field perspectives (structure/process, quadrant perspectives, the historical perspective, *looking as* and *looking at*) in relation to the gestalt process. This provides a tool for identifying states and approaching an understanding and a description of their complexity as a basis of relevant interventions in treatment and therapy settings, but also in educational, organisational, and political settings. This provides a tool for creating a systematic approach to the role of lifestyle (broadly viewed) in relation to mental health, as Walsh (2011) has called for. In the following, we discuss this point and put it into perspective.

Quadrant logic, community, and society

Through organismic self-regulation, the individual ascribes meaning to, and influences, his or her environment, and in this process the environment also co-shapes the individual. These field aspects are inextricably linked. It is important for this self-regulation to experience meaningfulness and coherence in the four quadrant perspectives: to be able to think and feel (UL), and act (UR) in a context where one is able to influence one's own conditions (LR) and participate in shared meaning making (LL).

Community psychology is traditionally a field-orientated approach based on an ecological perspective (Rappaport, 1977). Community-level efforts to optimise the exchange of "services" (LR) among local entities and organisations also include efforts to achieve enhanced awareness (UL) of living conditions (LR) in order to enable activation and mobilisation of the local population, often with a view to action (right-side quadrants) aimed at gaining greater influence on one's own conditions and optimising them. This process promotes the development of a new culture (LL), which says that "we can achieve change when we act together", that is, an experience of having a shared agenda, identity, and influence on one's own life.

Community psychology forms a basis for interventions that works in a concrete fashion with aspects in the lower-right quadrant in order to optimise aspects in the lower-left quadrant as part of enhancing the individual's (upper quadrants) and community's (lower quadrants) consciousness and actions (see, e.g., Berliner, 2004).

This approach, or intervention method, may also be relevant in relation to socially marginalised groups. An example is the Fountain House clubhouse model for people with mental disorders (Doyle et al., 2013; Sonne, 1984). One of the pillars in this model is that the person has a real experience of having a job identity. Unlike many social psychiatric initiatives, which typically operate on an individual level (upper quadrants), this model characteristically revolves around societal structures (LR). The model makes it possible to match the person's motivational regulation style (UL) with workplace demands and possibilities defined by society (LR). The model also promotes a culture that promotes the participants' sense of belonging (LL). This enables the person to establish a relationship with the meaning dimensions that are associated with having a job identity in our society. Therefore, the treatment/educational approach appears more as socially de-stigmatising and preventative reintegration work than merely as treatment (Sonne, 1985). The point is that the specific measures in the lower-right quadrant are implemented with consideration for the difficulties of the specific target group; thus, from all the quadrant perspectives, the person becomes a natural part of the societal whole. This stands in contrast to the pathologisation that due to widespread quadrant absolutism (from an exterior singular perspective) makes it difficult for some people to fit into the general social and cultural contexts.

This relates to the broader question of what form of government and what types of institutions (LR) we need in general, if we are to create viable conditions for human growth and well-being, development, and co-existence (LL, UL, UR). How can we, also on the larger scale of society, strive to promote development with optimally balanced coherence in the four quadrant perspectives? How should schools, care facilities, youth institutions, and workplaces be designed and organised to provide optimal settings for accommodating and promoting people's qualified self-determination in the regulation and management of their needs for autonomy, competence, relatedness, and meaning (see Tønnesvang, 2012b)?

The quadrant model clarifies the need for political decision makers to understand that it is both unproductive and obsolete to work from a single quadrant perspective (for example, economic concerns, LR) without incorporating the developmental potential and limitations in the domains of the other quadrants. We have to include conditions in as many quadrants as possible, and we should explicitly specify to what extent we exclude other quadrant aspects. The IGP approach does not involve knowing everything about what it is *possible* to observe and consider at all times in all four quadrant perspectives. The ambition is less utopian and simply involves installing a fundamental quadrant understanding in relation to one's work and considering the individual aspects of one's work from this holistic perspective, with the awareness that one engages in methodological reductions when restricting one's work to specific components of the quadrant whole.

A general positive consequence of applying the quadrant model as a way of experiencing, considering, and acting in the world is that it helps us see when *misunderstandings and conflicts can be explained by a confusion of perspectives*, where something pertaining to *one* quadrant perspective is mistakenly seen as the reason for something pertaining to another quadrant perspective. This makes it easier to notice when causal links are posited between things that are really just a differentiation of perspectives. For example, the finding that "people with less education have shorter life expectancies than people with more education" can be conveyed and perceived as a statement of cause and effect, implying that if we raise the general level of education, we will also increase longevity. From a quadrant perspective, however, it is natural to request an opening of the unreflected aspect of this argument. The cause might, instead, lie in the UR quadrant perspective in the form of individual constitutional genetic factors that, regardless of context, give some people a higher degree of resilience that is reflected both in increased longevity and higher educational attainment.

Statistical correlation is not the same as statistical causality. Finding correlations between two factors does not, in itself, explain what is the cause of what; neither does it explain where and how the most relevant intervention would be. When arbitrary correlations of various perspectives on a given reality give rise to erroneous conclusions, misconceptions, and misinterpretations from people with the power to implement initiatives based on these arbitrary correlations, the consequences for their surroundings can be most unfortunate.

The message of this book is that the quadrant model and the integrative attention to human gestalt dynamics can be relevant in relation to influencing (controlling) development in public and private organisations and institutions as well as in society at large. We propose that systems administrators, politicians, and decision makers with perspective awareness and a qualified capacity for integrative perspective taking will be better equipped to address the development of society and institutions on every level, including educational institutions (for example, schools, tertiary education, day-care facilities, and services for marginalised youth), care for the elderly, disability services, and the healthcare sector. A concrete use of the quadrant model in these contexts would facilitate qualified questions about what characterises settings, rules, contracts, economic conditions, and management (LR) that promote or hinder the performance of core services in relation to culture creation, community building, and appreciation (LL), well-being, mentality, values, and competence (UL) as well as physical expression, behaviour, and physical condition (UR).

From an IGP perspective, we will certainly question whether increasing levels of control and management in public organisations correlate with the transformational objectives that would be established based on quadrant reflection if the goal is to develop systems that are capable of addressing (near and distant) future challenges. Such future-attuned systems will probably benefit from being reinvented in an atmosphere of trust, mutuality, and respect at all levels (Laloux, 2014) carried forward by transformational leaders (Bass & Reggio, 2006) who understand the relevance of raising their awareness and being sensitive to what is emerging (Scharmer, 2007).

Health and disease in the quadrant perspectives

If we view the issue of disease and health in the perspective of the quadrant model, here, too, we can put a variety of perspectives on these concepts into play. The frame of reference for distinctions between disease and health that the individual's own experience (UL) offers might be very different from the frame of reference that comes from what is objectively measurable with regard to disease *vs.* health (UR). In addition, we are dealing with society's (LR) and the discursive–cultural (LL) attribution of meaning to the conceptual pair that provides the meaning-making context in relation to what we mean by healthy or sick, and what measures should be taken in this regard.

When public sector areas are unclear in relation to the quadrant differentiations, some of the possible consequences are as follows.

- Social workers managing politically decided cost cuts (LR) in the effort to bring more people on to the labour market wind up fighting against citizens and healthcare workers managing variations of individual concerns in upper-quadrant perspectives.
- There are states of disease/health characterised by lack of congruence—and possibly conflict—between the four perspectives. That is the case, for example, with some of the more recent diagnoses, such as fibromyalgia and a lifestyle disease such as obesity.
- We seek to overcome limitations in our capacity to analyse and understand complex conditions, for example, by labelling them as "psychosomatic" (which often involves a fuzzy combination of aspects from the singular quadrants), "functional diseases", or "lifestyle diseases" (a label that refers somewhat vaguely to interacting aspects from the singular and plural quadrant perspectives).
- There might be an exaggerated pathologisation of human life management. It makes a difference, for example, whether we view a person's behaviour from a psychiatric/medico-social or an anthropological, sociological, or psychological perspective (see also Brinkmann, 2010).

There might be a wide variety of professional, economic, and commercial interests associated with the prioritisation of perspectives. Some of these interests might place a greater emphasis on certain quadrants, tending towards quadrant absolutism. For example, the pharmaceutical industry could have a general interest in having certain types of behaviour and life management defined as diseases (UR). In a positive light, this makes it possible to offer treatments, but it can also cause the conditions that are labelled as "diseases" to be locked into an upper-right quadrant perspective. Similarly, the oft-heard view that psychological conditions should be viewed in the same light as somatic conditions could lead to a higher degree of recognition of these conditions, but it might also lead to an unnecessary pathologisation of phenomena whose complexity are really better understood with the inclusion of the three other quadrant perspectives. That could be the sort of situation we are facing with regard to the so-called functional diseases and the issue of whether they should be understood in the light of their functional status in a complexity of perspectives or as organic (UR) diseases. It might similarly be relevant in relation to our understanding of other conditions, for example, stress and some of the conditions that are currently diagnosed as depression or ADHD (Jørgensen, 2012).

While critical awareness in relation to the previous examples address an overly one-sided UR perspective, we see a case of a one-sided LL perspective in connection with the growing problem of obesity with the clear focus on bringing about a change of attitude by means of information campaigns. If we instead supplement the left-side quadrant perspectives with a quadrant look at what *contributed* to the growing problem of obesity, there are key issues to be identified in the lower-right quadrant that might call for action. For example, the physical access to products that increase obesity has become ever easier and less costly in recent decades (larger bags of sweets, larger bottles of soft drinks, cheaper alcohol, etc.). In addition, factors that limit physical activity have increased, for example, in the form of additional television channels and more hours of television, as well as the proliferation of computers, the Internet, car ownership, escalators, etc.

From a quadrant point of view, the challenges we are facing here could be addressed politically with *initiatives that make it easier to make healthier choices*. What would it mean for the general health level of the population, *if* it was not disproportionately more expensive to buy a small bag of sweets than a large container, and *if* it was not disproportionately more expensive to buy a small soft drink than a large one, and *if* it took more effort to go to the escalator than to the stairs? In our organismic self-regulation, we tend to choose the easiest solution (like the "default" setting on a computer). Therefore, if we want to create a society that promotes health, it might be effective to make healthier choices more accessible and unhealthy choices less accessible. This means that politicians have to operate in the lower-right quadrant perspective with regulations and control. One example of this is the smoking ban that was passed not long ago, making it more difficult, overnight, to be a smoker.

These regulations might be viewed as unreasonable infringements of personal freedom, but the point is that the *experience* of individual freedom (UL), when viewed from the point of view of the right-side quadrant perspectives, is already fundamentally framed by biological facts, physiological limitations, and life conditions (including death, the concern for the common good, and the state of the planet). That is why existential philosophers associate the concept of freedom with responsibility in relation to existential conditions. In connection with this point, it is a question of how we create the political regulations that best promote qualified existential self-regulation, and when we fail by not making these regulations. *This is where the quadrant rationale should be considered.* Viewed from the lower-right quadrant, individual freedom is framed by concern for others, common ground rules, and concern for other exterior factors and limitations (the climate, etc.). As a metaphor and a parallel, it would be absurd to claim that the rules governing soccer place unreasonable restrictions on the players and inhibit their personal initiative.

The key is to optimise the balance between, on the one hand, the experience of individual freedom (UL) and action potential (UR) and, on the other hand, shared values (LL), ground rules, and relations to other people (LR).

Personal responsibility in the sense of the individual's efforts to take responsibility for himself and his life (in an existential sense) should not be mixed up with the political decision-makers' responsibility to develop optimal structures for society (LR) and consider how these interact with aspects from the other quadrant perspectives.

Political views and perspective takings

If we apply the quadrant perspectives to some of the key differences between the political left and right, we find that these differences also relate to the relative emphasis on perspectives. When presented with a person who is poor, for example, a person on the political right will typically focus on the person's individual responsibility (UL) and initiative (UR) with regard to changing his situation, while a person on the political left will focus more on the possibilities in the context (LR and LL) that the person has and has had with regard to being able to change his situation. One wing will focus more on the individual perspective (the organism), while the other will focus more on the systems/relational perspective (the environment). We cannot claim that one perspective is fundamentally more relevant than the other, but politics is often characterised by a polarisation of views that could instead be recognised as meaningful disagreement and complexity in perspective takings. With the mass media as active contributors, this happens to a degree where the struggle between the polarities tends to overshadow the possible integration of perspective complexity. It would be more helpful if the media (especially the public service media) would pursue the principle of balanced reporting in an effort to increase the complexity of perspective takings rather than focusing on particularised differences as a conflict theme. It would also be positive if leading politicians would make an effort themselves to raise the level of the debate to an issue of differences in perspective and *meaningful disagreement* instead of perpetuating a rigid polarisation of viewpoints (equivalent to frozen gestalt dynamics).

Another aspect of development is that mobile phones, the Internet, and social media have given us a level of global access to information that is extreme in comparison with what we had in the past. Twitter and Facebook are tools in uprisings against dictatorships. Change seems to be happening more rapidly than we have seen in the past. Many see this as an advantage, but perhaps sometimes the changes are happening too rapidly: they are certainly not without costs. With the concept of development that is presented in this book (as transformation processes that involve identification, dis-identification, and reintegration), the question is to what extent dissociation processes occur when a society moves (too) quickly from one level to another.

The quadrant model, with its access to a structured and nuanced understanding of the many different perspectives that we can apply to human meaning making, is also helpful in seeking to understand the interactions of diverse cultures and religions (LL), climate changes and different forms of government (LR), racial and physiological differences (UR), and individual differences in mentality (UL) that characterise the peoples of the earth. A renewed socio-psychological interest in man's social character (LL) in a quadrant perspective will, thus, focus explicitly on the way in which the social character is promoted and developed by various economic control mechanisms and forms of government (LR) and produces a certain form of mental organisation on the level of the individual (UL) and its associated typical forms of individual behaviour (UR) and social interaction (LR). Since capitalism is the overall prevailing economic system in the world, and, thus, provides certain general lower right quadrant premises for human living (seen from all quadrants), it would be interesting to explore consequences (as seen from all four quadrant perspectives) of alternative forms of socio-economic organisation. Nowadays, there are only few initiatives or experiments in this respect (see, e.g., Hancox, 2013).

The challenge for the coming years involves applying our huge insight into, and recognition of, differences in perspective taking optimally. Bringing awareness to the many perspectives (identifying them) will be the first step in that direction and (according to the paradoxical theory of change) also the most important step. As long as one remains identical with one's own (ego-related or ethnocentric) perspective, one cannot identify it, and, consequently, one also cannot dis-identify with it. Assuming that our own perspective is the right one locks us into our own limited perspective taking. For example, a nation may believe that it is its duty, in the name of democracy, to intervene in a foreign culture, which might, in fact, be undergoing levels of development from a completely different point of departure. An intervention might result in cultural dissociation in the form of a civil war between polarised groups in the country the nation set out to "save" in its own name. It is essential to understand what it means that different cultures undergo different levels of development at different rates (LL), to avoid causing a quadrant clash by forcing a form of government on a cultural character that is not in a position to benefit from the given form of government.

Closing remarks: IGP as an individual integrative life practice

Anyone can use IGP as a practical tool in relation to his or her own life management. By bringing awareness to life processes and life conditions in the four quadrant perspectives and by focusing on one's own self-regulation and gestalt processes, one can help oneself uncover field relations as a basis for more situationally adequate—and, thus, also more proactive—existentially competent action.

In a sense, one can sharpen one's focus on where and how it is most appropriate to respond (= taking responsibility) in the regulation of one's intrinsic/extrinsic motivation.

If, for example, one has decided to take on a practical life project, the quadrant perspectives can help clarify how aspects in the four domains interact, and where and how (in which quadrant) it is most meaningful to make an effort. Furthermore, attending to one's own gestalt inclination (that is, *looking at* one's own patterns) can sharpen one's awareness in determining which domain should be one's personal focus area. If one has a tendency, for example, to act in a way that is so quick that it is maladaptive (UR), it might be helpful to build a personal practice (UR) that promotes better contact with an experience (UL) of inner centring and calm to act in ways that resonate more deeply with one's being.

The key is to train one's ability to use IGP as a personal and professional tool in one's life and work practice, for example, by engaging in a training practice that promotes the development of what we call *qualified quadrant awareness*.

IGP awareness training and exercises

The *analytical* approach to understanding the mutual relations and interactions of the quadrant perspectives includes uncovering what one may, in fact, discover from each of the four perspectives on the given phenomenon. The analytical approach provides an intellectually differentiated awareness from all four quadrant perspectives, which also includes the different phenomenological realities of the involved individuals.

The *contemplative* approach, which involves focused in-depth reflection by means of techniques such as meditation and mindfulness training, is another way of striving to attain awareness of the underlying complexity of the different fragmentations and dichotomies as well as their integrative nature and relatedness. This approach can facilitate better contact with *what is*. The contemplative approach is based on Eastern wisdom and a thousand-year-long tradition involving various meditative practices. Through focused reflection, IGP awareness exercises (see Exercise Boxes 4 and 5 below) seek to combine the two complementary approaches (the analytical and the contemplative).

In the book's section on awareness, it was described how awareness and mindfulness training can promote the acknowledgement of facts and of *what is,* also going beyond the common dichotomous and dualist mind-sets. In the section on energy and the body's energy field, we also addressed aspects of the contemplative approach. In a sense, Zen, field theory, and fundamental discoveries in the gestalt approach, such as the concept of isomorphism in gestalt psychology, the role of the concept of awareness for the integration of complexity and complementarity, and concepts such as "creative indifference" and "the paradoxical theory of change" all support and indicate the meaningfulness of working specifically with awareness training.

Meditative practice, above all, is fundamental awareness training. It can take place on different levels of reflection and awareness, and it can involve the body to varying degrees. A simple form of awareness meditation may, for example, be to sit with a straight back while bringing awareness to one's breathing, acting simply as an *observing witness* to one's own flow of awareness. In a non-judging, accepting manner, one observes what is: emotions, thoughts, images, body sensations. Regardless of what comes into one's awareness, one accepts it without remaining identical with it. As mentioned earlier in the book, that means identifying with it and, subsequently, dis-identifying with it.

The following is a similarly simple form of meditation, which focuses on breathing. It is a thousand-year-old Tibetan form of meditation that brings awareness to one's breathing and the body (upper-right quadrant), thus sharpening one's attention on the moment:

EXERCISE BOX 3

Stress-reducing breathing meditation*

Think the first word(s) as you inhale and the next word(s) as you exhale.

Do this for a few minutes for each word pair.

in—out

deep—slow

body calm—body light and comfortable

smile to the body—body completely relaxed

this moment—a unique moment

*You can find this as an audio-guided exercise at gestalt.dk/exercises.

Through meditation generally, you train your ability to separate from your identification (or fusion) with what comes into awareness: thoughts, emotions, and material binds. In a sense, you train your capacity for *defusion* instead of *fusing* with the *content* of consciousness.

This form of meditation also trains what is called a *witness function*, which involves loosening oneself from the environmental or field context and getting into contact with oneself as context. In the ACT approach, this is known as *self as context*, which is similar to being in a defused contact relationship with oneself instead of something else in the field. It can best be explained as the field being *essentially* reduced to one's own organism. When we say *essentially*, it is because this meditative practice may, in fact, also be experienced as an opening to gaining contact with the field as such.

In IGP, when we speak of meditative processes (and processes in general), we do so in their relationship with the energetic field aspect. According to field theory, as mentioned earlier, we are all "of the field", and expanded awareness that not only concerns what might be called the "body-self" (see, e.g., Kepner, 2001), but also what might be called "the energy body", or "the body's energy field", might, therefore, provide access to contact with the energy field as such. That this has not yet been made measurable in a scientific sense does not mean that we cannot experience it by practising energy exercises, meditation, and contemplative life practice.

In the present context, we shall not go into the traditions that more specifically address this energy field and the subtle energy in connection with meditation and self-development, and we also shall not offer more detailed instructions as to how we believe the specific energy exercises with reference to these traditions can be part of the practical IGP work. In a Danish context, Bob Moore (Mauthner & Mauthner, 1992), among others, has offered inspiration for possible ways of engaging this field. His teaching has influenced developments in a number of psychotherapy schools (see, e.g., Bertelsen, 1982; Boadella, 1987; Gamborg, 1999; Haldrup et al., 2007; Vedfeldt, 1996). With the concept of the working energy field, with its energy streams, energy points, energy centres (chakras), and levels of energy fields (auras), Moore has suggested ways of working with subtle energy in an organismic context. This type of energy work reflects several of the points that are also crucial in IGP, as shown in the following example.

The understanding of how awareness is used as a tool to loosen "lumps" in the energy flow.

The concept of the creative dynamics of the polarity and complementarity relationship, which, in Moore's understanding is also manifested in the positive and negative currents in the energy flow (a parallel to electricity).

The importance of operating with a holistic "of the field perspective" where the energy concept can be meaningful for approaching a better understanding of complexity.

Energy exercises can involve focusing one's awareness (from a *looking as* perspective) on the specific energy centres and energy streams of the organism in order to enable an identification with lumps, also known as blockages, in the natural energy flow. This awareness process, which may trigger emotions, body reactions, images, and thoughts, can, in itself, make blockages dissolve, which, in turn, leads to a more natural energy flow. Moore has described energy exercises as a way of working into *the subtle anatomy* in order to resolve blockages.

Another type of meditative practice that might be helpful for reaching beyond the dichotomy that is also perpetuated by language is to meditate on words that, in themselves, promote a more profound contact with fundamental human values—so-called *values of first order* (Ryan et al., 2008). This could include words such as responsibility, acceptance, trust, forgiveness, love, honesty. Meditating on such a word will bring one into profound contact with these particular values and with the polar and complementary properties that are, in a dynamic sense, aspects of these values (such as mistrust, etc.).

Meditation, for example as described above and perhaps in combination with meditation on one of the aforementioned words or a topical theme, can be used as a daily routine—a sort of daily exercise in mental hygiene, like brushing one's teeth. As always with hygiene, discipline is essential.

An introduction to a meditation exercise might go as follows:

Do not produce thoughts, but instead accept what comes. This might be thoughts or fragments of thoughts, it might be emotions or images, or might be simply a body reaction.

(continued)

Our thoughts tend to be rational, so it is quite likely that thoughts will emerge such as "What's the purpose of this?", "I don't think I'm very good at this", etc., or that your thoughts will turn to completely different issues: "Wonder what's for supper", etc.

When you notice these thoughts, do not fight them, but let go and let them pass without following them, exactly as if you were standing by the side of the road, a bus pulls up, and you are not getting on that bus right now; just let it pass.

In the same way, try to just register the thoughts that come and go—let them pass by you—and let whatever else comes into your flow of awareness pass by. Register it without having to follow it. If you find it difficult to do, you are on the right path.

It takes practice to be able to accept whatever comes into one's awareness without becoming identical with it. Thoughts, especially, have a tendency to pull us in.

The accepting stance in meditation also contains the difficult paradox that we sometimes have to accept our inability to accept. The point is that acquiring the capacity for acceptance is a way of accepting *what is* in order to break free from being caught up in it—for example, in one's thoughts.

Personal IGP training practice involves working deliberately with "cross-training". That means engaging in intellect training, spiritual training, shadow training, and body training, corresponding to the four modules in *Integral Life Practice*: mind, spirit, shadow, and body modules (Wilber et al., 2008).

Intellect training (mind) is primarily about training one's capacity for perspective takings. Spiritual training (spirit) can include a meditation practice, for example. Shadow training (shadow) means identifying one's gestalt inclination, and, in addition to psychotherapy, it may also include, for example, dream work, etc. Body training (body) may involve various forms of sports as well as working on a more subtle body level, for example, through yoga. Naturally, many practices relate to several of these modules at the same time, such as physical activity combined with a certain form of awareness, for example, meditative hiking or subtle karate, both of which contain the combination of body and spirit work. Each person has to find his or her own optimal combination, but it is more beneficial to do a moderate amount of work in all four domains than a great deal of work in just one.

In our work with the quadrant model, we have developed a number of special IGP awareness exercises that incorporate the concept of the field perspective. These are focused reflection exercises that can also help the practitioner identify and dis-identify with a fixed gestalt inclination and promote more flexible and situationally adequate gestalt dynamics. The exercises integrate the approach of analytical quadrant logic with the meditative path to recognising the full complexity. The exercises relate to the *mind*, the *spirit*, and the *shadow* module (see above).

Below, we present three IGP awareness exercises and an exercise for working with both the self-regulation wave and the quadrant model.

EXERCISE BOX 4

*IGP awareness training**
As with the other meditation and focused reflection exercises, you should find a setting where you will not be disturbed. You should carry out the exercise slowly and with a focused presence. The ellipses indicate places where you should take your time to simply be open to whatever you come into contact with.

- Sit in a relaxed position with a straight back, close your eyes . . .
- Now attend to the four quadrant perspectives. Perhaps you can imagine standing in the middle of a large field.
- When you look around, behind you to one side, you have the interior singular quadrant perspective: your thoughts, emotions, experiences, and what you are familiar with as your old patterns . . .
- Behind you to the other side, you have the exterior singular quadrant perspective: your body, body symptoms, biological processes, your actions, and your behaviour . . .
- In front of you to one side lies the exterior plural quadrant perspective: the contexts you are a part of (at work, in your personal life), other people, and all the systems, organisations, regulations, and laws that you are part of and subject to . . .
- To the other side in front of you are the interior aspects of these factors, for example, the different moods or atmospheres in the different relations you are a part of . . .
- Now move around these four quadrant perspectives at your own pace and see what you discover . . .
- Now move back to the centre . . .

(continued)

- Imagine taking a lift down—back in time. Get off at a floor much further down—maybe in your childhood. Again, move around in each of the four quadrants at that time and see what you discover . . .
- Return to the centre, and take the lift back up to where you began.
- Now imagine that you are moving up into a helicopter perspective, where you see everything from slightly above. Just be curious, and notice if any connections show up in or among the quadrant perspectives . . . also in relation to then and now . . .
- See what comes up if you meditate on this for a few minutes . . .
- Return, and open your eyes.

*You can find this as an audio-guided exercise at gestalt.dk/exercises.

EXERCISE BOX 5

IGP awareness training

- Think back in your life to pleasant and joyful experiences . . . Dwell on one of them . . . and imagine that you are back in that situation, so that you can sense it right now in the four quadrant perspectives . . .

In that situation, notice the context as seen from the lower-right quadrant perspective . . . Where are you? . . . Who else is present? . . . What is going on? . . .

From the lower-left quadrant perspective . . . What is the shared and joint experience? . . .

From the upper-right quadrant perspective . . . What is your behaviour, and what is your purely bodily reaction in the situation? . . .

And from the upper-left quadrant perspective . . . What are you feeling, and what are you thinking? . . .

Notice how you experience that your psychological needs for autonomy, competence, relatedness, and meaning are satisfied . . . how you are nourished—getting the psychological oxygen you need . . .

Take that feeling with you into what we call the here and now . . . and move further up . . . have a sense that reaches slightly into the future . . . now meditate a few minutes . . . is there a first step that calls for being taken? . . . Just see what comes up . . .

Come back now, and open your eyes.

*You can find this as an audio-guided exercise at gestalt.dk/exercises.

EXERCISE BOX 6

IGP awareness training*

- Sit in a relaxed position with a straight back.
- Pay attention to your breathing . . .
- Imagine that you are looking from the upper-right quadrant perspective in a *looking at* perspective: see yourself, as you are sitting right now, see details in your body . . . and also imagine that you are able to observe all the body processes and the inner organs . . .
- Stay with the upper-right quadrant perspective and go to a *looking as* perspective: Imagine that you *are*, in a way, your body from the inside . . . Notice how this imperceptibly and automatically moves you into the upper-left perspective and how you actually sense and notice this feeling in your body . . . Now try to sense your own centring and a deeper contact with yourself . . . a feeling of really being able to be who you are . . . Feel your intrinsic psychological needs . . . your need for autonomy . . . your need for relatedness and contact with others . . . your competence and your ability to do the things you need to be able to do . . . your sense of direction and meaning in your life . . .
- Now notice the transition from the upper to the lower quadrant perspectives . . . Feel your skin, which separates you from what is not you—the environment . . .
- Now bring attention to the two lower quadrants; first the lower-right quadrant: the system contexts you are a part of . . . the relations you interact with; then the lower-left quadrant: the sensation and atmosphere in the various relational contexts . . . Notice to what extent and how your intrinsic needs for autonomy, competence, relatedness, and direction are being met and receive—or fail to receive—the optimal amount of psychological oxygen . . .
- Now move into a helicopter perspective; see the whole thing from above, and be open to whatever comes up . . . perhaps something calls for some sort of action on your part . . .

*You can find this as an audio-guided exercise at gestalt.dk/exercises.

As another type of exercise in relation to the two basic models that have been presented in the book, the quadrant model and the self-regulation model (the self-regulation wave), we close by introducing a practical personal exercise that enhances the understanding of the relationship between the quadrant perspective taking and the gestalt process in organismic self-regulation.

EXERCISE BOX 7

Exercise for working with the self-regulation model and the quadrant model in a Looking At perspective

- Try to plot your own profile in relation to the self-regulation wave (Figure II, p. 53), ideally focusing on a particular issue that you are dealing with. Where do you see your main blockages as you move through your typical self-regulation or gestalt process, from sensation to clarity, energy mobilisation, action, contact with your target goal, and withdrawal? Where in the process do you tend towards too much inhibition, and where do you tend towards not enough inhibition?
  - How do you make sense of this?
  - Is it related to your old patterns?
  - What/who might help you loosen/change them?
- Now try to fill out the quadrant schema, focusing on the same issue. In each of the fields, write down what you notice from each of the perspectives. Now be curious about relations in the four perspectives of the field and the mutual relations of the current situation, the history of the field, and your gestalt inclination (your old patterns).
- Now try to relate the two models to each other. How is the movement in your self-regulation wave, for example, related to the structural aspect in the upper-left quadrant perspective? If you are curious about the history of the field, for example, the system contexts (lower quadrants) that you were part of in your childhood, how might you relate that to the structural aspect in the upper-left quadrant and to the fluctuations in your self-regulation wave?

Integrative methodological pluralism

I n the following, we describe Wilber's (2006) distinction between inside perspectives (process) and outside perspectives (structure) in each of the four quadrants. Just as we distinguish between process and structure in all the quadrants (as described in the section on p. 22), Wilber distinguishes between inside and outside aspects in all the quadrants. While the terms *exterior* and *interior* in the quadrant mind-set thus refer to the right and left sides of the quadrant model, respectively, *outside* and *inside* refer to different perspectives that can be applied in each of the four quadrants. This is illustrated in Figure 21.

Wilber uses the eight resulting zones to specify eight prototypes of research methodology in their respective links to the object area that they serve to explore. This is illustrated in Figure 22.

In Zone 1, we find the inside of the interior singular perspective, which involves the perceived states one has at given points in time. These states correspond to the process aspect in our terminology and are explored prototypically with a phenomenological or contemplative methodology. Zone 2 concerns the outside in the interior singular perspective and refers to the mental organisational patterns (structures) that a person is the bearer of. While experiences of mental states

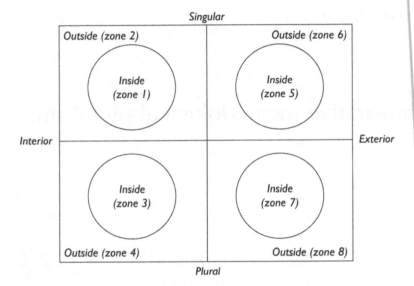

Figure 21.   Research methodological prototypes
(adapted from Wilber, 2006, p. xx).

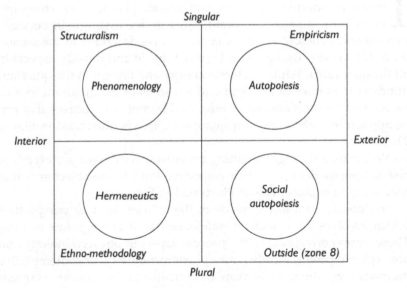

Figure 22.   The eight zones of the quadrant model
(adapted from Wilber, 2006, p. xx).

are a Zone 1 phenomenon (process), the mental organisation that structures these experiences is a Zone 2 phenomenon (structure). The prototypical methodology for exploring Zone 2 conditions is structuralism. Thus, while a phenomenological method is used to explore direct experiences as "the feel of an I" (Zone 1), a structuralist method is used for uncovering "the look of the I", corresponding to the organisational patterns that connect phenomena in their experience (Zone 2).

Zone 3 (in the interior plural quadrant) refers to the inside of the interior plural and, in many regards, corresponds to Zone 1 (in the interior singular), except that this concerns inside phenomena in relation to the interior plural: attachment and we-ness in the form of shared experiences of meaning ("the feel of a we"), which can be made the object of hermeneutic studies or be explored though participatory practices.

Similarly, Zone 4 (interior plural) in many regards is parallel to Zone 2 (interior singular), in the sense that Zone 4 concerns the cultural organisational patterns, implicit forms of life, and other forms of tacit shared knowledge, language games, logics, and discourse rules that (like "the look of a we") frame the essential ways in which individuals in various cultures and groups are able to experience shared understanding, we-ness, and attachment. For example, individualist or collectivist cultural patterns (Triandis, 1995) frame the border definitions of both individuals and in-group/out-group formations in different ways.

Of the four zones concerning the exterior forms of the individual and the collective, Zone 5 (inside of the exterior singular) essentially corresponds to Zone 7 (inside of exterior plural), while Zone 6 (outside of exterior singular) corresponds to Zone 8 (outside of exterior plural). Zone 6 concerns the positivist empirical uncovering of objectively observable factors, and Zone 8 concerns the positivist empirical charting of the outward-functional relations of systems. Both these zones refer to familiar focus areas and methodological approaches in scientific circles and, therefore, require no further explanation.

It might be relevant to describe Zones 5 and 7 in a little more detail, however. They refer to the insides of the exterior of, respectively, the individual, and the collective. Thus, in principle, Zones 5 and 7 pertain to factors that can be observed objectively (by use of the senses or technological instruments—for example, a scanner in the exterior singular quadrant). The unique quality of Zones 5 and 7 is that they are based on exterior and objectively given data, but in such a way that they concern the inside functionality of the exterior data. An example might be the objective uncovering of the perceptual or neurocognitive processes that are at play when a researcher relocates a frog's eyes, as Maturana and Varela (1987) did, to study how the frog subsequently navigates in the world. The point is *not* the phenomenological experience of what it *is like, per se*, to be the frog in this condition. The point is to study how the perceptual or neuro-cognitive processes in the frog's behaviour *objectively* appear from the point of view of these processes (if they could be seen to have a point of view). Maturana and Varela contributed to the opening of Zone 5 concepts and methodology with their *autopoiesis thinking*, which today is associated in particular with *cognitive science*. The methodological prototype in Zone 7 (exterior plural) corresponds to *social autopoiesis*, as described by Luhmann (1995) in particular, in the inside functionality of social systems centred on communication.

As a further, doubling specification of the four quadrants, the eight zones, according to Wilber, describe the possible perspectives that can be applied to any event. Seen in total, they constitute the basis of inte-grative perspectivism with its related methodologies. Integrative science cannot be limited to just some of the zones, but requires a so-called *integrative methodological pluralism* that includes *all* the zones, and which can form a contextualising basis for any methodological reductions one might apply in carrying out specific research studies in one or more of the quadrants. As mentioned earlier, the distinction between structure and process largely corresponds to Wilber's distinc-tion between outside and inside in both the interior and the exterior quadrant perspectives. It should also be mentioned that what we call integrative methodological pluralism is, in Wilber's terms, integral methodological pluralism.

NOTE

1. Kegan's (1982, 1994) model of development includes six developmental stages. The fundamental template is based on the duality (not the dualism) between subject and object. The point is that on each level, the object is identical with the subject on the previous stage. Development, thus, results from a process where specific aspects of the person that are perceived as identical with who the person is (unconscious aspects of the subject) become conscious aspects of the person (each aspect becoming one of many objects). For example, when a person develops from the interpersonal stage (corresponding to Kegan's stage 3) to the institutional stage (stage 4), the unconscious, controlling focal point of interpersonal relationships and connections has become a conscious aspect that can more easily be made the object of a deliberate choice, and which has been replaced by the unconscious, controlling focus on identity and ideology. If/when the development continues, a similar movement takes place from what was previously identical with the subject—and, hence, invisible— to something visible that is added as a basis of ongoing development. For each developmental stage, it is possible to relate gradually to increasingly complex issues. (We are grateful to James Hammink for contributing this information.)

REFERENCES

Abbass, A. A., Kisely, S. R., Town, J. M., Leichsenring, F., Driessen, E., De Maat, S., Gerber, A., Dekker, J., Rabung, S., Rusalovska, S., & Crowe, E. (2014). Short-term psychodynamic psychotherapies for common mental disorders. *Cochrane Database, 7.*

Andersen, T. (1991). *The Reflecting Team: Dialogues and Dialogues about the Dialogues.* New York: W. W. Norton.

Bass, B. M., & Riggio, R. E. (2006). *Transformational Leadership* (2nd edn). Mahwah, NJ: Lawrence Erlbaum.

Bateman, A., & Fonagy, P. (2006). *Mentalization-Based Treatment for Borderline Personality Disorder.* Oxford: Oxford University Press.

Baumeister, R. F., & Tierney, J. (2011). *Will Power: Rediscovering the Greatest Human Strength.* New York: Penguin.

Beisser, A. (1971). The paradoxical theory of change. In: J. Fagan & I. Shepherd (Eds.), *Gestalt Therapy Now: Theory, Techniques, Applications* (pp. 77–80). Highland, NY: Gestalt Journal Press.

Beisser, A. (1990). *Flying Without Wings: Personal Reflections on Being Disabled.* New York: Bantam Books.

Berliner, P. (Ed.) (2004). *Fællesskaber – en Antologi om Community Psykologi* [Communities – An Anthology on Community Psychology]. Copenhagen: Frydenlund.

Bertelsen, J. (1982). *Drømme, chakrasymboler og meditation* [Dreams, chakra symbols and meditation]. Copenhagen: Borgen.

Beutler, L. E. (2009). Making science matter in clinical practice: redefining psychotherapy. *Clinical Psychology: Science and Practice, 16*(3): 301–317.

Beutler, L. E., Engle, D., Mohr, D., Daldrup, R. J., Bergan, J., Meridith, K., & Merry, W. (1991). Differential response to cognitive, experiential and self directed psychotherapeutic procedures. *Journal of Consulting and Clinical Psychology, 59*: 333–340.

Black, T. G. (2008). Applying AQAL to the quantitative/qualitative debate in social sciences research. *Journal of Integral Theory and Practice, 3*(1): 1–14.

Blankertz, S. (2004). Beratung, Therapie und Coaching mit dem neuen "Gestalttypen-Indikator" (GTI) [Counselling, therapy and coaching with the new "gestalt type indicator" (GTI)]. *Gestaltkritik, 1*. Accessed at: www.gestalt.de/blankertz_gestalttypen_indikator_gti.html.

Boadella, D. (1987). *Lifestreams: An Introduction to Biosynthesis*. London: Routledge.

Bohr, N. (1961). *Atomic Theory and the Description of Nature*. Cambridge: Cambridge University Press.

Brinkmann, S. (Ed.) (2010). *Det diagnosticerede liv – sygdom uden grænser* [The Diagnosed Life – Illness without Limits]. Aarhus: Klim.

Buber, M. (1937). *I and Thou*. New York: Charles Scribner's Sons.

Burley, T. (2012). A phenomenologically based theory of personality. *Gestalt Review, 16*(1): 7–27.

Burley, T., & Freier, C. M. (2004). Character structure: a gestalt–cognitive theory. *Psychotherapy, Theory, Research, Practice, Training, 41*(3): 321–331.

Burley, T., Resnick, B., & Resnick, R. (2005). *Explanatory Notes for Gestalt Process Diagnosis*. Santa Monica, CA: Gestalt Associates Training Los Angeles (GATLA).

Clarkson, P. (2011). *Gestalt Counselling in Action*. London: Sage.

Clarkson, P., & Mackewn, J. (1993). *Fritz Perls*. London: Sage.

Conduit, E. (1987). Davanloo in Britain. *Changes: An International Journal of Psychology and Psychotherapy, 5*(2): 333–337.

Conrad, K. (1958). *Die beginnende Schizophrenie, Versuch einer Gestaltanalyse des Wahns* [Emergent Schizophrenia. Attempts at a Gestalt Analysis of Psychosis]. Stuttgart: Georg Thieme.

Csikszentmihályi, M. (1998). *Finding Flow: The Psychology of Engagement with Everyday Life*. New York: Basic Books.

Damasio, A. (1994). *Descartes' Error: Emotion, Reason, and the Human Brain*. New York: Putnam.

Damasio, A. (1999). *The Feeling of What Happens: Body, Emotion and the Making of Consciousness.* London: Heinemann.

Deci, E. L., & Ryan, R. M. (2000). The 'what' and 'why' of goal pursuit: human needs and the self-determination of behavior. *Psychological Inquiry, 11*: 227–268.

Deci E. L., Koestner, R., & Ryan, R. (1999). A meta-analytic review of experiments examining the effects of extrinsic rewards on intrinsic motivation. *Psychological Bulletin, 125*(6): 627–668.

Deurzen-Smith, E. (2012). *Existential Psychotherapy and Counselling in Practice.* London: Sage.

Diener, M. J., Hilsenroth, M. J., & Weinberger, J. (2007). Therapist affect focus and patient outcomes in psychodynamic psychotherapy: a meta-analysis. *American Journal of Psychiatry, 164*(6): 936–941.

Divine, L. (2009). Looking AT and looking AS the client. The quadrants as a type structure lens. *Journal of Integral Theory and Practice, 4*(1): 21–39.

Doyle, A., Lanoil, J., & Dudek, K. J. (2013). *Fountain House: Creating Community in Mental Health Practice.* New York: Columbia University Press.

Ecker, B., & Hulley, L. (1996). *Depth-oriented Brief Therapy: How To Be Brief when You Were Trained To Be Deep and vice versa.* San Francisco, CA: Jossey-Bass.

Ecker, B., & Hulley, L. (2007). *Coherence Therapy Practice Manual & Training Guide.* Oakland, CA: Pacific Seminars.

Ecker, B., & Toomey, B. (2008). Depotentiation of symptom-producing implicit memory in coherence therapy. *Journal of Constructivist Psychology, 21*(2): 87–150.

Falk, B. (2010). *At være der hvor du er* [Being where You Are] (3rd edn). Copenhagen: Nyt Nordisk Forlag Arnold Busck.

Favrholdt, D. (2009). *Filosoffen Niels Bohr* [Niels Bohr the Philosopher]. Copenhagen: Informations.

Feldenkrais, M. (1972). *Awareness through Movement.* New York: Harper & Row.

Folensbee, R. W. (2007). *Neuroscience of Psychological Therapies.* Cambridge: Cambridge University Press.

Fowler, J. W. (1981). *Stages of Faith: The Psychology of Human Development and the Quest for Meaning.* San Francisco, CA: Harper & Row.

Freud, S. (1923). *The Ego and the Id. S. E., 19*: 12–66. London: Hogarth Press, 1961.

Friedländer, S. (1918). *Schöpferische Indifferenz.* Munich: Georg Müller.

Gamborg, H. (1999). *Det Usynlige i Helbredelse* [The Invisible in Healing]. Copenhagen: Forlaget Olivia.

Gendlin, E. (1981). *Focusing*. New York: Bantam Books.

Gergen, K. J. (1994). *Realities and Relationships: Soundings in Social Construction*. Boston, MA: Harvard University Press.

Gibson, J. J. (1979). *The Ecological Approach to Visual Perception*. Boston, MA: Houghton Mifflin.

Gilbert, P. (Ed.) (2005). *Compassion. Conceptualisations, Research and Use in Psychotherapy*. London: Routledge.

Graves, C. W. (1970). Levels of existence: an open system theory of values. *Journal of Humanistic Psychology, 10*(2): 131–155.

Greenberg, L. (2002). *Emotion Focused Therapy: Coaching Clients to Work through Feelings*. Washington, DC: American Psychological Association.

Habermas, T., & Bluck, S. (2000). Getting a life: the emergence of the life story in adolescence. *Psychological Bulletin, 126*: 748–769.

Haldrup, A., Thorup, H., & Møller Kristensen, D. (2007). *Mød livet fra kernen* [Meeting Life from the Core]. Aarhus: Specular.

Hancox, D. (2013). *The Village Against the World*. London: Verso.

Hansen, J. T. (1997). Egenvilje er ikke fri vilje. [Own volition is not free will.] *Journal of Anthropological Psychology, 2*: 56–62.

Hansen, J. T. (2001a). *Selvet som rettethed: en teori om noget af dét, der driver og former menneskeliv* [The Self as Directedness: A Theory about what Drives and Forms Human Lives]. Aarhus: Forlaget Klim.

Hansen, J. T. (2001b). Gestaltterapi Som Relationel, Psykodynamisk og Strukturel Teori og Terapitilgang [Gestalt therapy as a relational, psychodynamic, and structural theory and therapy approach]. *Matrix: Nordisk Tidsskrift for Psykoterapi*. Copenhagen: Dansk Psykologisk.

Harris, R. (2008). *The Happiness Trap*. London: Constable & Robinson.

Hart, S. (2008). *Brain, Attachment, Personality: An Introduction to Neuroaffective Development*. London: Karnac.

Hayes, S., & Smith, S. (2005). *Get Out of Your Mind and Into Your Life. The New Acceptance and Commitment Therapy*. Oakland, CA: New Harbinger.

Hayes, S., Strosahl, K., & Wilson, K. (2003). *Acceptance and Commitment Therapy. An Experiential Approach to Behavior Change*. New York: Guilford Press.

Heidegger, M. (1962). *Being and Time*. New York: Harper & Row.

Heller, L., & LaPierre, A. (2012). *Healing Developmental Trauma*. Berkeley, CA: North Atlantic Books.

Hofmann, S. G., Sawyer, A. T., Witt, A. A., & Oh, D. (2010). The effect of mindfulness-based therapy on anxiety and depression: a meta-analytic review. *Journal of Consulting and Clinical Psychiatry, 78*(2): 169–183.

Hostrup, H. (2010). *Gestalt Therapy*. Copenhagen: Museum Tusculanum Press.

Hunt, J. (2009). Transformational conversations. The four conversations of integral coaching. *Journal of Integral Theory and Practice*, 4(1): 69–92.

Jacobs, L. (2011). Critiquing projection: supporting dialogue in a post Carthesian world. In: T. Bar-Yoseph Levine (Ed.), *Gestalt Therapy: Advances in Theory and Practice (Advancing Theory in Therapy)* (pp. 81–91). London: Routledge.

Johnson, S., & Greenberg, L. (1985). Emotionally focused couples therapy: an outcome study. *Journal of Marital and Family Therapy*, 11: 313–317.

Johnson, S., & Smith, E. W. L. (1997). Gestalt empty chair dialogue versus systematic desensitization in the treatment of a phobia. *Gestalt Review*, 1: 150–162.

Jørgensen, C. R. (2012). *ADHD: Bidrag til en kritisk psykologisk forståelse* [ADHD: Contribution to a Critical Psychological Understanding]. Copenhagen: Hans Reitzel.

Kabat-Zinn, J. (1993). Mindfulness meditation: health benefits of an ancient Buddhist practice. In: D. Goleman & J. Garin (Eds.), *Mind/Body Medicine*. Yonkers, New York: Consumer Reports.

Kabat-Zinn, J. (2005). *Coming to Our Senses*. New York: Hyperion.

Kegan, R. (1982). *The Evolving Self—Problem and Process in Human Development*. Cambridge, MA: Harvard University Press.

Kegan, R. (1994). *In Over Our Heads: The Mental Demands of Modern Life*. Cambridge, MA: Harvard University Press.

Kellogg, S. H. (2014). *Transformational Chairwork. Using Psychotherapeutic Dialogues in Clinical Practice*. New York: Roman and Littlefield.

Kempler, W. (1981). *Experiential Psychotherapy with Families*. London: Brunner-Routledge.

Kepner, J. I. (2001). *Body Process. A Gestalt Approach to Working with the Body in Psychotherapy*. Santa Cruz, CA: Gestalt Press.

Kierkegaard, S. (1965). *Skrifter i udvalg*. [Selected Texts]. Copenhagen: Gyldendal.

Kohlberg, L. (1969). *Stages in the Development of Moral Thought and Action*. New York: Holt, Rinehart, & Winston.

Köhler, W. (1925). *The Mentality of Apes*. New York: Harcourt Brace.

Kohut, H. (1977). *The Restoration of the Self*. New York: International Universities Press.

Kreiman, G., Koch, C., & Fried, I. (2000). Imagery neurons in the human brain. *Nature*, 408: 357–361.

Kupfer, D. J., First, M. B., & Regier, D. A. (2002). *A Research Agenda for DSM-V*. Arlington, VA: American Psychiatric Association.

Lakoff, G., & Johnson, M. (1980). *Metaphors We Live By*. Chicago, IL: University of Chicago Press.

Laloux, F. (2014). *Reinventing Organizations: A Guide to Creating Organizations Inspired by the Next Stage of Human Consciousness*. Brussels: Nelson Parker.

Levine, P. A. (2005). *Healing of Trauma*. Boulder, CO: Sounds True.

Lewin, K. (1951). The field approach: culture and group life as quasi-stationary processes. In: W. L. French, C. Bell, & R. Zawacki (Eds.), *Organization Development and Transformation. Managing Effective Change* (pp. 112–113). New York: McGraw-Hill.

Lewin, K. (1952). *Field Theory in Social Science: Selected Theoretical Papers*. London: Tavistock.

Loevinger, J. (1976). *Ego Development*. San Francisco, CA: Jossey-Bass.

Lowen, A. (1967). *The Betrayal of the Body*. New York: Collier Books.

Lowen, A. (1977). *Bioenergetics*. New York: Penguin Books.

Luhmann, N. (1995). *Social Systems*. Stanford, CA: Stanford University Press.

Maturana, H. R., & Varela, F. J. (1987). *The Tree of Knowledge: The Biological Roots of Human Understanding*. Boston: Shambhala.

Mauthner, A., & Mauthner, A. (Eds.) (1992). *Conversations with Bob Moore*. Kirchdorf, Switzerland: Private publication.

McAdams, D. P. (1993). *The Stories We Live By: Personal Myths and the Making of the Self*. New York: Guilford Press.

McCullough, L., & Magill, M. (2009). Affect-focused short-term dynamic therapy: empirically supported strategies for resolving affect phobias. In: R. A. Levy & S. J. Ablon (Eds.), *Handbook of Evidence-Based Psychodynamic Psychotherapy* (pp. 249–278). Totowa, NJ: Humana Press.

Merleau-Ponty, M. (1962). *Phenomenology of Perception* (Part 1). New York: Humanities Press.

Nohria, N., Groysberg, B., & Lee, L.-E. (2008). Employee motivation—a powerful new model. *Harvard Business Review, July–August*: 78–84.

O'Leary, E. (Ed.) (2013). *Gestalt Therapy Around the World*. Oxford: Wiley-Blackwell.

Perls, F. (1969). *Ego, Hunger and Aggression*. New York: Vintage Books.

Perls, F. (1972). *Gestalt Therapy Verbatim*. New York: Bantam Books.

Perls, F. (2006). Four lectures. In: J. Fagan & I. Shepherd (Eds.), *Gestalt Therapy Now. Theory, Techniques, Applications* (pp. 14–38). Highland, NY: Gestalt Journal Press.

Perls, F., Hefferline, R. F., & Goodman, F. S. (1973). *Gestalt Therapy. Excitement and Growth in the Human Personality*. London: Pelican Books.

Piaget, J. (1937). *The Origins of Intelligence in Children*. London: Routledge.

Piet, J., & Hougaard, E. (2011). The effect of mindfulness-based cognitive therapy for prevention of relapse in recurrent major depressive disorder: a systematic review and meta-analysis. *Clinical Psychology Review*, 31(6): 1032–1040.

Polster, E. (1987). *Every Person's Life is Worth a Novel*. New York: W. W. Norton.

Polster, E. (1995). *A Population of Selves*. San Francisco, CA: Jossey-Bass.

Polster, E., & Polster, M. (1973). *Gestalt Therapy Integrated*. New York: Vintage Books.

Rappaport, J. (1977). *Community Psychology: Values, Research, & Action*. New York: Holt, Rinehart & Winston.

Rasmussen, T. H. (1996). *Kroppens filosof, Maurice Merleau-Ponty* [Maurice Merleau-Ponty, the Philosopher of the Body]. Copenhagen: Semiforlaget.

Reich, W. (1980). *Character Analysis*. New York: Farrar, Straus & Giroux.

Robson, C. (2011). *Real World Research* (3rd edn). Chichester: Wiley.

Roediger, H. L. (1990). Implicit memory: retention without remembering. *American Psychologist*, 45(9): 1043–1056.

Rubin, E. (1915). *Synsoplevede Figurer: Studier i Psykologisk Analyse (Første Del)* [Visually Experienced Figures: Studies in Psychological Analysis (part one)]. Copenhagen: Gyldendalske Boghandel, Nordisk.

Ryan, R. M., & Deci, E. L. (2000). Self-determination theory and the facilitation of intrinsic motivation, social development, and well-being. *American Psychologist*, 55(1): 68–78.

Ryan, R. M., Huta, V., & Deci, E. L. (2008). Living well: a self-determination theory perspective on eudaimonia. *Journal of Happiness Studies, 9*: 139–170.

Ryan, R. M., Lynch, M. F., Vasteenkiste, M., & Deci, E. L. (2011). Motivation and autonomy in counseling, psychotherapy, and behavior change: a look at theory and practice. *The Counseling Psychologist*, 39(2): 193–260.

Ryff, C. D., & Singer, B. H. (2008). Know thyself and become what you are: a eudaimonic approach to psychological well-being. *Journal of Happiness Studies*, 9(1): 13–39.

Sartre, J.-P. (1948). *Existentialism and Humanism*. London: Methuen.

Schachter, D. L. (1987). Implicit memory: history and current status. *Journal of Experimental Psychology: Learning, Memory, and Cognition*, 13(3): 501–518.

Schafer, R. (1996). *Handlesprog og fortælling*. Copenhagen: Det lille.

Scharmer, C. O. (2007). *Theory U: Leading from the Future as It Emerges.* Cambridge, MA: The Society for Organizational Learning.

Segal, Z. V., Williams, J. M. G., & Teasdale, J. D. (2002). *Mindfulness Based Cognitive Therapy for Depression: A New Approach to Preventing Relapse.* New York: Guilford Press.

Sharps, M. J., & Wertheimer, M. (2000). Gestalt perspectives on cognitive science and on experimental psychology. *Review of General Psychology,* 4(4): 315–336.

Sheldrake, R. (1989). *The Presence of the Past: Morphic Resonance and the Habits of Nature.* New York: Viking.

Siegel, D. J. (1999). *The Developing Mind: Toward a Neurobiology of Interpersonal Experience.* New York: Guilford Press.

Smuts, J. (1926). *Holism and Evolution.* New York: Macmillan.

Sonne, M. (1984). Fountain House modellen, rehabilitering af kronisk sindslidende [The Fountain House model, rehabilitation of the chronic mentally ill]. *Nordisk Psykologi,* 36(2): 75–90.

Sonne, M. (1985). *Dansk Psykologforenings Betænkning om Distriktspsykiatri* [The Danish Psychological Association's Report on Community Psychiatry]. Copenhagen: Dansk Psykologforening.

Spagnuolo Lobb, M., & Amendt-Lyon, N. (Eds.) (2003). *Creative License: the Art of Gestalt Therapy.* Vienna: Springer.

Staemmler, F. (2006). A Babylonian confusion? On the uses and meanings of the term 'field'. *British Gestalt Journal,* 15(2): 64–83.

Staemmler, F. (2009). *Aggression, Time and Understanding.* New York: Routledge.

Stern, D. N. (1985). *The Interpersonal World of the Infant.* New York: Basic Books.

Stevens, J. O. (1971). *Awareness: Exploring, Experimenting, Experiencing.* Palo Alto, CA: Real People Press.

Strümpfel, U. (2004). Research on gestalt therapy. *International Gestalt Journal,* 27(1): 9–54.

Tashakkori, A., & Creswell, J. W. (2007). The new era of mixed methods. *Journal of Mixed Methods Research,* 1(1): 3–7.

Tashakkori, A., & Teddlie, C. (1998). *Mixed Methodology: Combining Qualitative and Quantitative Approaches.* Thousand Oaks, CA: Sage.

Taylor, C. (1991). *The Malaise of Modernity.* Toronto: House of Anansi Press.

Teasdale, J. D. (1993). Emotion and two kinds of meaning: cognitive therapy and applied cognitive science. *Behavior Research and Therapy,* 31(4): 339–354.

Teasdale, J. D. (1999). Emotional processing, three modes of mind and the prevention of relapse in depression. *Behaviour Research and Therapy*, 37(Suppl. 1): 53–57.

Teasdale, J. D., Pope, M., Moore, R. G., Haywurst, H., Williams, S., & Segal, Z. V. (2002). Metacognitive awareness and prevention of relapse in depression: empirical evidence. *Journal of Counselling and Clinical Psychology*, 70(2): 275–287.

Tønnesvang, J. (2002). *Selvet i pædagogikken: selvpsykologiens bidrag til en moderne dannelsespædagogik* [The Self in Educational Settings: A Self-psychological Contribution to a Modern Theory of Education]. Aarhus: Forlaget Klim.

Tønnesvang, J. (2012a). Identity, self, and motivation: steps towards an integrative approach. *Nordic Psychology*, 64(4): 228–241.

Tønnesvang, J. (2012b). Grundlag for en pædagogisk dannelsestænkning: kvadrantlogik, vitaliseringsmiljø og kvalificeret selvbestemmelse [Foundation for a pedagogical theory on *Bildung*: quadrant logic, vital-ising milieus, and qualified self-determination]. In: J. Tønnesvang & M. S. Ovesen (Eds.), *Psykologisk Ilt i Pædagogisk og Organisatorisk Arbejde: Praksisudvikling på Grundlag af Integrativ Selvpsykologi* [Psychological Oxygen in Pedagogical and Organisational Work: Practice Development Based on Integrative Self Psychology] (pp. 27–88). Aarhus: Forlaget Klim.

Tønnesvang, J. (2015). Dannelse og kompetence – kvalificeret selvbestem-melse som grundlag for pædagogik, undervisning og samarbejde [*Bildung* and competence – qualified self-determination as a frame-work for understanding pedagogy, teaching and cooperation]. In: J. Klitmøller & D. Sommer (Eds.), *Læring, Dannelse og Udvikling* [Learn-ing, *bildung*, and development] (pp. 151–183). Copenhagen: Hans Reitzels.

Tønnesvang, J., & Hedegaard, N. B. (2014). *The Vitalizing Model – An Introduction.* http://klim.dk/bog/psykologisk_ilt.htm

Tønnesvang, J., & Nielsen, T. B. (2006). Psykologisk ilt i lederskabsrela-tioner [Psychological oxygen in leadership relations]. *Psyke & Logos*, 27(2): 767–803.

Tønnesvang, J., Sommer, U., Hammink, J., & Sonne, M. (2010). Gestalt therapy and cognitive therapy – contrasts or complementarities? *Psychotherapy, Theory, Research, Practice, Training*, 47(4): 586–602.

Toomey, B., & Ecker, B. (2007). Of neurons and knowings: constructivism, coherence psychology and their neurodynamic substrates. *Journal of Constructivist Psychology*, 20(3): 201–245.

Törneke, N. (2010). *Learning RFT: An Introduction to Relational Frame Theory and its Clinical Applications*. Reno, NV: Context Press.

Triandis, H. C. (1995). *Individualism and Collectivism*. Boulder, CO: Westview Press.

Tulving, E. (1985). Memory and consciousness. *Canadian Psychology, 26*(1): 1–12.

Vedfeldt, O. (1996). *Bevidsthed* [Counsciousness]. Copenhagen: Gyldendal.

Walsh, R. (2011). Lifestyle and mental health. *American Psychologist, 66*(7): 579–592.

Watson, J. C., & Bedard, D. L. (2006). Clients' emotional processing in psychotherapy: a comparison between cognitive–behavioral and process–experiential therapies. *Journal of Consulting and Clinical Psychology, 74*: 152–159.

Wertheimer, M. (1997). Laws of organization in perceptual forms. In: W. D. Ellis (Ed.), *A Sourcebook of Gestalt Psychology* (pp. 71–88). Highland, NY: Gestalt Journal Press.

White, M. (2006). *Narrativ Praksis* [Narrative Practice]. Copenhagen: Gyldendal Akademisk.

Wilber, K. (1995). *Sex, Ecology, Spirituality: The Spirit of Evolution*. London: Shambhala.

Wilber, K. (2000). *Integral Psychology: Consciousness, Spirit, Psychology, Therapy*. London: Shambhala.

Wilber, K. (2003). *Kosmic Consciousness* (audio book). Boulder, CO: Sounds True.

Wilber, K. (2006). *Integral Spirituality. A Startling New Role for Religion in the Modern and Postmodern World*. London: Shambhala.

Wilber, K., Patten, T., Leonard, A., & Morelli, M. (2008). *Integral Life Practice*. Boston, MA: Integral Books.

Wilson, K. (2008). *Mindfulness for Two—An Acceptance and Commitment Therapy Approach to Mindfulness in Psychotherapy*. Oakland, CA: New Harbinger.

Winnicott, D. W. (1971). *Playing and Reality*. London: Tavistock

Worsfold, K. E. (2009). The body clinical cognitive theory: from Beck to mindfulness. *Contemporary Buddhism: An Interdisciplinary Journal, 10–2*: 220–240.

Yalom, I. D. (1980). *Existential Psychotherapy*. New York: Basic Books.

Yontef, G. (1993). *Awareness, Dialogue & Process. Essays on Gestalt Therapy*. New York: Gestalt Journal Press.

Yontef, G., & Jacobs, L. (2008). Gestalt therapy. In: R. J. Corsini & D. Wedding (Eds.), *Current Psychotherapies* (pp. 1–71). New York: Thomson Brooks/Cole.

Zeigarnik, B. (1997). On finished and unfinished tasks. In: W. D. Ellis (Ed.), *Sourcebook of Gestalt Psychology* (pp. 300–314). New York: Humanities Press.

Zinker, J. (1977). *Creative Process in Gestalt Therapy*. New York: Vintage Books.

INDEX